CIM REVISION CARDS

Analysis and Evaluation

John Williams of Marketing Knowledge

GW00728770

ELSEVIER

BUTTERWORTH
HEINEMANN

AMSTERDAM • BOSTON • HEIDELBERG • LONDON • NEW YORK • OXFORD
PARIS • SAN DIEGO • SAN FRANCISCO • SINGAPORE • SYDNEY • TOKYO

Butterworth-Heinemann is an imprint of Elsevier
Linacre House, Jordan Hill, Oxford OX2 8DP
30 Corporate Drive, Suite 400, Burlington, MA 01803

First published 2006

Copyright © 2006, Elsevier Ltd. All rights reserved

No part of this publication may be reproduced in any material form (including photocopying or storing in any medium by electronic means and whether or not transiently or incidentally to some
other use of this publication) without the written permission of the copyright holder except in accordance with the provisions of the Copyright, Designs and Patents Act 1988 or under the terms of a
licence issued by the Copyright Licensing Agency Ltd, 90 Tottenham Court Road, London, England W1T 4LP. Applications for the copyright holders written permission to reproduce any part of this
publication should be addressed to the publisher

Permissions may be sought directly from Elsevier's Science & Technology Rights Department in Oxford, UK: phone: (+44) (0) 1865 843830, fax: (+44) (0) 1865 853333,
e-mail: permissions @ elsevier.co.uk. You may also complete your request on-line via the Elsevier homepage
(http://www.elsevier.com), by selecting 'Customer Support' and then 'Obtaining Permissions'.

British Library Cataloguing in Publication Data
A catalogue record for this book is available from the British Library

Library of Congress Cataloguing in Publication Data
A catalogue record for this book is available from the Library of Congress

ISBN-13: 978-0-7506-6766-1
ISBN-10: 0-7506-6766-4

For information on all Butterworth-Heinemann publications visit our web site at http://books.elsevier.com

Printed and bound in Great Britain

06 07 08 09 10   10 9 8 7 6 5 4 3 2 1

Working together to grow
libraries in developing countries

www.elsevier.com | www.bookaid.org | www.sabre.org

TABLE OF CONTENTS

PREFACE

Welcome to the CIM Revision Cards from Elsevier/Butterworth–Heinemann. We hope you will find these useful to revise for your CIM exam. The cards are designed to be used in conjunction with the CIM Coursebooks from Elsevier/Butterworth–Heinemann, and have been written specifically with revision in mind. They also serve as invaluable reviews of the complete modules, perfect for those studying via the assignment route.

■ Learning outcomes at the start of each chapter identify the main points

■ Key topics are summarized, helping you commit the information to memory quickly and easily

■ Examination and revision tips are provided to give extra guidance when preparing for the exam

■ Key diagrams are featured to aid the learning process

■ The compact size ensures the cards are easily transportable, so you can revise any time, anywhere

To get the most of your revision cards, try to look over them as frequently as you can when taking your CIM course. When read alongside the Coursebook they serve as the ideal companion to the main text. Good luck – we wish you every success with your CIM qualification!

INTRODUCTION TO ANALYSIS AND EVALUATION

Unit 1

LEARNING OUTCOMES

In this unit you will:

➡ Appreciate the role of marketing in adding value

➡ Understand the importance of market orientation in determining the success of an organization (see syllabus)

➡ Understand the range of tasks involved in undertaking rigorous evaluation and analysis

➡ Review the strategic process and understand the importance of analysis and evaluation within it

➡ Understand the motivation behind the Professional Postgraduate Diploma Analysis and Evaluation syllabus

➡ Gain an overview of the main approaches to situational analysis and evaluation

➡ Appreciate the role of marketing within the strategic planning process.

Formulating strategy

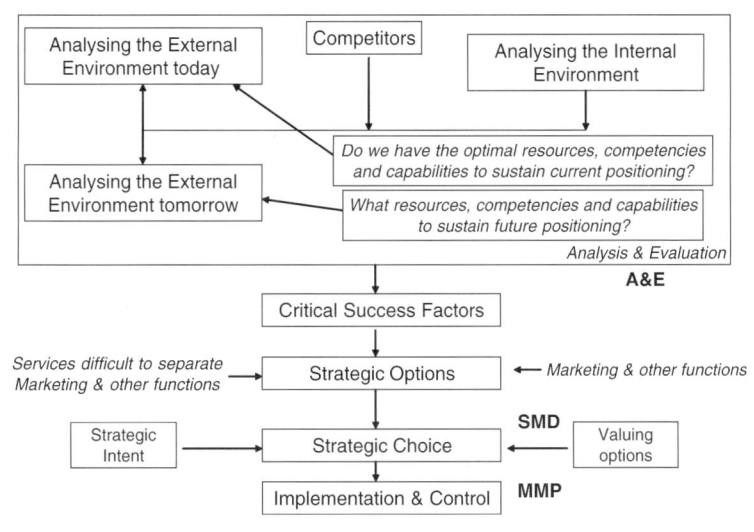

KEY DEFINITIONS

Market orientation involves the specific activities that translate the philosophy of marketing into practice

Customer orientation involves understanding customers well enough to create superior value for them continuously

Competitor orientation is the awareness of the capabilities of competitors

Interfunctional co-ordination involves the company using all its resources to create value for its target customers

Analysis, represents a method for gaining information relating to external markets and internal assets

Evaluation – is the study of options in the light of company capabilities and attitude to risk

This unit looks at:

- Business orientation and the role of marketing – identifying the business intelligence needed to inform strategy-making in domestic and international markets
- Assessing the impact of major trends in the global context on strategy making
- Conducting a strategic audit of the internal and external environment, including an evaluation of business performance, using appropriate tools, models, analysis of numerical data and management information
- Appraising the nature of culture within organizations and the importance of its fit with strategy and operations
- Synthesizing a coherent and concise assessment of the situation facing an organization and developing alternative scenarios

ELEMENT 1
Strategic management and the role of marketing
10%

ELEMENT 2
Evaluation of business performance
30%

ELEMENT 3
Analysis of the internal environment
20%

ELEMENT 4
Analysis of the external environment
20%

ELEMENT 5
Characteristics of the global marketplace
20%

Marketing philosophy

■ Markets are becoming increasingly competitive and dynamic. The main driver behind the marketing concept is the belief that organizations are more likely to succeed if they are focused on the customer.

Market orientation

■ Narver and Slater have identified different components of market orientation. At the core is a focus on *long-term profits*. The business needs to be *sustainable* and have a *strategic perspective* rather than a tactical one. This should be supported by an *organizational culture* that encourages all employees to promote customer satisfaction. This should be underpinned *by customer orientation*, *competitor orientation* and *inter-functional co-ordination*.

Business Orientation

Key Questions

◦ What is the business orientation of this organization?
◦ To what extent is the organization finance/operations/people or market led?
◦ What is the significance of knowing a business orientation for marketers?
◦ How can a marketer best utilize this information to develop better plans?
◦ What is the role of marketing in firms displaying different orientations?
◦ Does marketing have a role in such organizations?

Operations	R&D	Marketing	Financial	People

Orientation	*Orientation*	*Orientation*	*Orientation*	*Orientation*
◦ Production orientated ◦ Dominated by operations department ◦ Principal role is to buffer/protect organization from external fluctuations	◦ Product orientated ◦ Design orientated ◦ Focus is on innovation ◦ Continuously attempting to be first with new or improved product or service features	◦ Principally customer orientated ◦ Recognizing that the customer is the only part of the business process which brings cash into the organization, everything else is a cost	◦ Principally focused on maximizing short-term profits ◦ Often at the expense of long term customer satisfaction ◦ Marketing is seen as an expense which needs to be controlled	◦ Principal belief is that employees are the cornerstone to satisfying external customers which, in turn, maximizes profitability ◦ Employees tend to be financial stakeholders

Fig. 1.1. *Formulating strategy* Remember what we are trying to achieve?

Operations	R&D	Marketing	Financial	People
○ Characterized by high volume, low variety production runs with long lead times and fixed production schedules	○ Objective is to be the first company to introduce new concept	○ Recognized in the ideal sense that Increasing company performance could be better achieved through satisfying customer needs and wants	○ Justifying long term investment in the building product and corporate brand reputation is difficult in such organizations as focus is on short term	○ Considerable employee motivation schemes – Job enlargement/Job enrichment strategies, job flexibility, maternity/paternity policies
○ Customer is limited in choice	○ Tends to lose ground over time to competitors who will imitate and improve basic concept introduce by innovators	○ As a business philosophy should drive all aspects of business, i.e. all functions should focus their activities on ensuring customer satisfaction	○ Still the dominant focus of most organizations in the UK and North America	○ Examples include a number of Danish companies, very few in the UK but John Lewis is probably a good example
○ Epitomized by Henry Ford as 'customers can have any colour as long as it is black'	○ Companies characterized by applying price skimming strategies to recoup high development costs	○ Initially concept included only external customers that influenced, financed and adopted products and services, later concept was broadened to include all stakeholders potentially influencing corporate success including internal customers	○ Examples of such organizations include Hanson	
○ Focus is dependent on what company makes	○ Example of such companies include Phillips, computer games and other software products, High fashion houses, restaurants and entertainment establishments, consultancy and other agency			
○ Marketing's role is mainly to regulate customer demand	○ Marketing plays a limited role in these organizations – entails researching new concepts and promotion			

Fig. 1.1. Continued

The different types of business culture are represented in Figure 1.3 and provide a framework to analyse and evaluate companies.

■ A study by Doyle, Wong and Saunders (1993) demonstrated that Anglo-Saxon companies such as those operating in North America and the United Kingdom were short-term in outlook by being more profit-oriented, whereas Japanese had a balanced orientation taking each business function into consideration and taking a longer-term business perspective. The study also indicated that simply adopting a pure marketing approach was not likely to improve performance as much as it would by applying a balanced approached depicted in

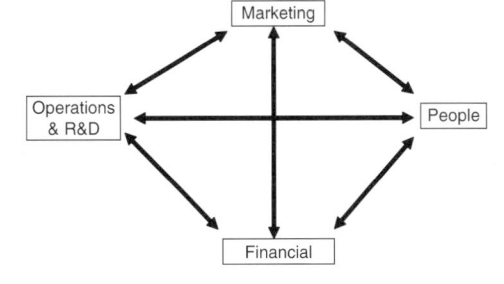

Fig. 1.2. Balanced orientation
Source: Adapted Doyle, Wong and Saunders

Marketing stakeholders

So far we have talked about three groups of stakeholders in the process of creating value: customers, competitors and employees. But other groups can influence the success of an organization. The seven markets model is shown in Figure 1.5.

The seven markets model

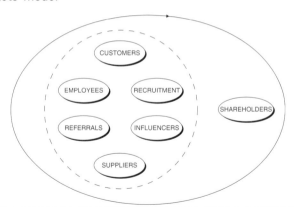

Effective marketing involves the realization that all stakeholders matter. They invest in the company and allow the business to invest in itself. But shareholders do not exist in a vacuum. There is overlap between the different groups. Employees may become shareholders, for example. Many companies have share schemes specifically to encourage this crossover.

Marketing and value

- Marketing has been criticized in the past for focusing solely on customer value largely ignoring other stakeholder groups

- Marketing needs to define value more broadly in terms of economic value – the idea that every activity should create a surplus, i.e., that outputs should have a higher value than inputs

- For marketing to be seen as relevant inside the business, marketing activities need to be seen as contributing to that profit by creating value not destroying it

- It is important to demonstrate how marketing adds value by using rigorous business metrics for all marketing activities. To show how activities add value, there is a need to be able to measure their contribution

The role of marketing in corporate strategy

Marketing needs to be at the core of corporate strategy. There are three important roles for marketing to fulfil in the planning process.

Identification of customer requirements

If a customer-orientated approach is adopted, there is a need to know as much as possible about who is buying the product or service. This will involve market research.

Competitive Positioning

Markets tend to be heterogeneous, i.e., they are made up of groupings that are similar to each other but differ in significant respects from other groups. The aim is to cluster these segments around the same need. Once this has been done, there is a need to find out how attractive the potential targets are, what are the requirements of that target, and what are our competencies to meet that requirement

Implementing the marketing strategy

Effective communication across organizational functions is critical for smooth implementation. This is even more important in service companies where the customer may have contact with several front line employees. Each must give a consistent message of what the company is about. These 'boundary spanners' (so-called because they span the boundary between the customer and company) are critical to the success of otherwise any service organization.

The role of analysis and evaluation in marketing planning

Managing the marketing planning process needs to begin with a thorough analysis of the company's situation. The company needs to analyse its markets and the marketing environment to evaluate potential opportunities and threats. The question 'Where are we now?' needs to be answered before moving on to decide where the organization wants to be, and how it is going to get there.

Summary

An analysis of the external and internal environment needs to be undertaken

External analysis covers customers, competitors, market, and macro environment.

Specifically:

Customer – segments, motivations and unmet needs

Competitors – identification, strategic groups, cost structures, strengths, weaknesses and competencies

Market – size, growth, profitability, entry barriers, cost structure, distribution networks, entry barriers and attractiveness

Macro environment – political, economic, social, demographic, cultural, environmental and legal

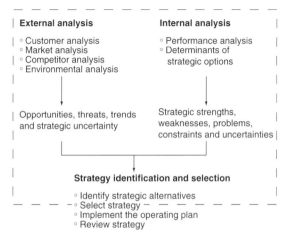

Fig 1.3. Overview of the strategic market management process
Source: Adapted from Aaker (1998)

Market orientation is strategic and concentrates on long-term performance. It emphasizes customer focus.

- Organizations need to understand their customers and competitors, not just an end in itself, but as a means of delivering shareholder value
- The marketing process should be interfunctional
- Analysis and evaluation are the essential foundation stones of an effective marketing strategy
- Detailed market research and analysis are essential to ensure that an organization makes the most of any opportunities
- Analysis and evaluation helps companies avoid potential risks or, as a minimum, ensures that they are prepared. A range of models exist to help structure the analysis
- An emphasis is placed on understanding the strategic implications of analysis
- Marketing needs to adopt a broad definition of value that embraces all stakeholder groups but emphasizes the importance of shareholders
- Marketing metrics is needed to ensure that marketing is seen as accountable. Rigorous analysis should be undertaken and information synthesized. This is followed by generation of strategic alternatives and their evaluation

Hints and tips

■ It is not sufficient to be able to describe a model, you also need to apply it to a particular context. At the end of a unit, or any activity, try to think of examples and commit them to memory

■ Another useful tip is to allocate your time in accordance with the number of marks allocated to a question. Even if you have a question that you could spend the whole three hours on, don't! It is easier to get the first few marks rather than the last few

■ It is also important to answer the question that is set. There is a danger, particularly in Section B, that students spend time telling the examiner all they know about a subject rather than focusing their answer on a particular context

■ It is worth spending a few minutes planning your answer before you start to write, so that the answer shows a logical train of thought

■ After each examination, the senior examiners write a report for the Chartered Institute of Marketing in which they discuss how the students coped with the examination and highlight any particular problems that have been experienced

■ Even though the Analysis and Evaluation unit is new, looking back at previous reports, for example for Planning and Control, can give you an insight into the sort of things the examiners look for

EVALUATING PERFORMANCE: MARKETING METRICS

Unit 2

LEARNING OUTCOMES

To analyse an organization, it needs to be viewed from several perspectives. This unit focuses on marketing measures and in this unit you will:

➡ Understand the quantitative techniques that can be used to evaluate business performance
➡ Examine customer measures
➡ Consider how to evaluate marketing activities

Having completed this unit you will be able to:

➡ Use the various marketing measures of performance appropriately
➡ Use the balanced scorecard
➡ Evaluate performance over current and historic business cycles
➡ Common language in business tends to be finance and it is used across a number of functions in order to measure the viability of different strategic options.

- Finance has tended to dominate the business decision-making landscape within organizations even though it provides only a limited measure of performance

- Financial quantification was seen as paramount for making decisions as well as controlling activities within firms through budgeting. This made life difficult for many marketing activities such as advertising, public relations and, more recently, corporate social responsibility as the link with these activities and financial performance is difficult to measure.

KEY DEFINITIONS

Objectives: the specific intended outcomes of a strategy.

The balanced scorecard is an analytical approach which links setting objectives and setting performance measures.

ROCE is Return on Capital Employed.

Marketing metrics are agreed units of marketing measurement and their application.

SMEs are Small Medium-sized Enterprises, that is companies which employ fewer than 250 employees.

Evaluating performance is a very important area. If we view the contribution of marketing as worthwhile within the organization, then we need to be able to justify it.

- There are quantitative measures available which allow us to assess how:

  - the company is performing in marketing terms

  - how we can value our marketing assets, in particular, our brands

  - how we can audit our marketing activities

Objectives

- Objectives tend to be set in a hierarchy. Corporate objectives precede functional objectives, which develop into operational objectives

Performance outcomes

- The most commonly used measures of performance are sales, usually in the form of market share, and profitability

- The relationship between share and profit is not at all clear cut

Market share

- It allows us to evaluate performance against the competition without the confounding factor of changes in the market size and growth rates

- Valuable though this measure is, there are a number of issues that need to be addressed before a meaningful analysis can be generated

Market definition

■ This is a balance between the extended market (e.g., food, snacks) and micromarkets (e.g., salt and vinegar flavoured crinkle cut crisps in 25 g packets). At one extreme, our share might be very small and at the other, we may command 100 per cent share

■ It is important to define it at the appropriate level for the task in hand. Once the market has been defined, we need to determine the most useful timescale over which to evaluate the share shifts

Timescale

■ It is important not to over react to short-term fluctuations, but to be responsive if there is a problem

■ The choice of timescale will depend on the product category. There are few categories where a daily analysis of share would be appropriate, but probably none where a five yearly review of share would be helpful

■ In many markets, some sort of smoothing of the data may be appropriate, such as using a Moving Annual Total

Volume and value

When examining market share, a distinction is needed between volume (units) and value (revenue). Each tells a different story and their interaction is important.

Is current market share a good predictor of future share? The PIMS (Profit Impact in Market Strategy) database is useful in this regard.

PIMS

PIMS (Profit Impact in Marketing Strategy) began as an appraisal technique in the American General Electric Company in the late 1960s, but has developed into a major longitudinal research and evaluation programme based at Harvard University

■ Results suggest a significant regression towards the mean, that is, high initial shares tend to decline and low shares to increase over time

■ Thus, pioneers (the first into a market) gain an early share advantage over followers in industrial markets, and consumer industries

■ After 20 years, this lead is reduced on average for both industrial and consumer markets (Robinson, 1988)

■ The probable explanation is that, as a market matures, product quality advantages deteriorate. Unless the leader can innovate continuously, the other competitors will necessarily catch up gradually. High profits earned by the leader also attract entrants, so the market is likely to become more competitive

Market share and profitability

■ The causal direction of the relationship between share and profit is unclear. Early share gains may be due to luck, or initially superior resources

■ First-mover advantages may or may not exist. What then happens over time depends on how well managers defend their positions and keep up-to-date with technology and the market

■ The current share may be the result of past profits, or may deliver future profits, or both (or, in some highly contested strategic groups, neither of these)

■ To be useful, market share must be gained in a way that competitors will find hard to copy

Profitability

- There is a need to decide what the objective is in determining profitability. Is it to make a comparison – between lines? Brands? Divisions? Countries? Companies?

- It is important to compare like with like, in making comparisons. Is it gross profit, that is, before costs; or net profit, that is, after costs? Or somewhere in between, that is, after fixed costs but before marketing costs? Or before tax? Or before tax and interest?

- The relative profitability of brands. Margins might be examined twice; profit after all costs including marketing expenditure, and then again at profits excluding marketing expenditure — to discover which brands are successful because of their marketing support

- Differences in the allocation of overheads may change the apparent profitability of products or firms

- Taking profitability alone, it may be the result of positional advantage. If costs are lower than that of competitors for equivalent quality, or a premium price can be charged because of superior customer benefits (and extra costs are less than the additional margin), then higher profits can be expected

The balanced scorecard

The balanced scorecard was developed in the early 1990s by Kaplan and Norton (1992, 1993). They suggest developing a balanced set of objectives alongside a coherent set of performance measures. A business needs to be looked at from four different perspectives:

1. Financial – See the organization from a share-holder's perspective and evaluate the success of its strategy and implementation.

2. Customer – Put yourself in the customer's shoes. What is important to the customer and how is your organization performing against their requirements?

3. Internal – What are the critical internal processes which allow an organization to meet customers' needs? What are the processes which create satisfaction or dissatisfaction?

4. Innovation and learning – To create value, an organization must be able to continuously innovate and learn. How does your organization handle this?

■ Strategic measures (or performance indicators) are set in each of these areas to provide an objective basis with which to evaluate and formulate strategy

■ The balanced scorecard widens the view that managers have, by making them look at the business from different perspectives. It forces them to examine inter relationships between processes and functional areas, and to ensure consistency between objectives

Figure 2.1 gives an idea of how the balanced scorecard might work within an organization.

	Strategic objectives	Strategic measures
Financial	Return on capital	ROCE
	Cash flow	Cash flow
	Profitability	Net margin
	Profitability growth	Volume growth rate vs industry
	Reliability of performance	Profit forecast reliability
		Sales backlog
Customer	Value for money	Customer ranking survey
	Competitive price	Pricing index
	Customer satisfaction	Customer satisfaction survey
Internal	*Marketing*	
	○ Product and service development	Pioneer percentage of product portfolio
	○ Shape customer requirement	Hours with customer on new work
	Manufacturing	
	○ Lower manufacturing cost	Total unit cost (vs competition)
	○ Improve project management	Safety incident index

Fig. 2.1. The balanced scorecard

	Strategic objectives	Strategic measures
	Logistics	
	○ Reduce delivery costs	Delivered cost per unit
	○ Inventory management	Inventory level compared to output
	Quality	Levels of rejects
Innovation and learning	Innovate products and services	Percentage revenue from pioneer products
	Time to market	Cycle time vs industry norm
	Empowered workforce	Staff attitude survey
	Access to strategic information	Strategic information availability
	Continuous improvement	Number of employee suggestions

Fig. 2.1. Continued
Source: After Kaplan and Norton (1992, 1993)

Hints and tips

The examiners will be looking at your breadth of knowledge. So you need to move outside of your own industry and experience. Make sure you do all the activities suggested in this text but that you also read beyond this text. Read the trade press, watch the business news and listen to relevant radio programmes. Be like a magpie, picking up new examples showing how businesses analyse their situation and then apply their findings.

BRAND VALUATION

Unit 3

LEARNING OUTCOMES

After completing this unit you will be able to:

➡ Understand the importance of seeing brands as assets
➡ Appreciate the benefits of brand valuation
➡ Compare the various methods of valuing brands
➡ Explain the drivers for valuing brands as assets.

Syllabus Reference: 2.1, 3.1–3.5

KEY DEFINITIONS

A brand is a distinguishing name and/or symbol (such as a logo, trademark or package design), which is intended to identify the goods or services of either one seller or a group of sellers, and to differentiate those goods or services from those of competitors

Brand equity is a set of assets and liabilities linked to a brand name and symbol that add to or subtract from the value provided by a product or service to a firm or that firm's customers

Some of the most important assets of a company are intangible

One of the focal points of marketing is applying an organization's capital to build brands to capture long-term financial value

Brands as assets

■ Since the 1980s brands have been increasingly regarded as assets to be valued in the same way that we might value plant and machinery. Some companies have gone to the extreme of adding brands to the balance sheet

■ An assessment of a brand's value will include inherently subjective judgements about market position, market prospects, the quality, and value of marketing support

Reasons for brand valuation

There are advantages to be weighed against the considerable risks:

Balance sheet benefits

The balance sheet provides a picture of where the company is at one moment in time.

Financial markets

If all brands were valued on a consistent basis, it would be far easier for outsiders to make judgements on the relative value of corporate assets.

Separability

For a brand valuation to be useful in the marketplace, there must be a boundary between the brand and the company's assets. This is not always the case.

Management information

The process of valuing a brand may force managers to adopt a more strategic approach. Strategic options can be evaluated against the brand valuation and an assessment can be made on future brand values.

Internal management benefits

Stephen King, the brands guru sees brand valuation as proclaiming the purpose of the company. Whilst this may be important for outside stakeholders such as analysts and shareholders, it can be used to inspire employees and act as a kind of mission statement.

Brand valuation

There are a number of factors which can be used to establish the value of a brand:

Historic cost

The sum of all the investment into the brand starting with research and development costs, and moving onto distribution costs and promotional investments.

Current or replacement cost

Current cost is the price that a third party would pay for a brand, which is theoretically at least the same as it would cost to establish a totally new brand. Difficulties arise here because of the infrequency of brand trading.

Future earnings potential

- This method has proven very popular since it removes some of the disadvantages listed above
- It calculates the future earnings or cash flow of a brand which after all forms the basis of the value to the owner. Normally, the current earnings are extrapolated and discounted to present values
- There are problems with this. First, it assumes that the market will never change. Secondly, there will be no new competitors. Thirdly, there will not be any changes in the macro environment

Incremental value added

■ Many companies use this as a basis for an internal
measure of brand equity. The price of the brand is
compared with the price of the generics in the
market. The added value is viewed as equivalent
to the brand's equity. This approach undervalues
mass-market brands which profit from sales
volume and hence economies of scale. Niche
brands with small market share will also be
overvalued

The Interbrand model

A framework is based on a combination of objective
and subjective inputs. The Interbrand model has
seven components of brand strength.

Component of brand strength	Weighting (%)	Comments
Market	10	This is a measure of market stability. Brands in market where consumer preferences are enduring would score higher, e.g. a detergent brand would score higher than a perfume or clothing brand, because these latter categories are more susceptible to fluctuations in consumer preference.
Stability	15	Long established brands in any market would normally score higher because of the depth of loyalty they command, e.g. Rolls-Royce would score higher than Lexus.
Leadership	25	A market leader is more valuable. It is a dominant force and its relative market position gives it power, e.g. Coca-Cola would outperform Pepsi on a global basis.
Profit trend	10	The long-term profit performance can be viewed as a measure of the brand's ability to remain contemporary and relevant consumers.
Support	10	Brands which receive consistent investment and focused support usually enjoy a stronger franchise. However, it is important to note that the quality of the support is as important as the quantity.

Fig. 3.1. Interbrand model of brand strength

Component of brand strength	Weighting (%)	Comments
Geographic spread	25	Brands that have proven international acceptance and appeal are inherently stronger than regional or national brands as they are less susceptible to competitive attacks and hence are more stable assets.
Protection	5	Securing full copyright protection for the brand under international trademark and copyright law allows for greater stability and encourages investment in the brand.

Fig. 3.1. Continued
Source: Interbrand (2004)

The outcome of this approach is a brand strength score. Interbrand takes earnings to be 3-year weighted average of post-tax profits. The relationship between brand strength and brand value follows a classic S-shaped curve:

- As a brand's strength increases from virtually zero (an unknown or new brand) in the market, its value increases slowly

- As a brand moves to a number one or number two weighting in its market or becomes internationally known, or both, there is an exponential effect on its value

- Once a brand is established as a powerful world brand, its value no longer increases at the same exponential rate even if the market share improves internationally

Hints and tips

- It is important to keep up to date with current trends in brand valuation. Make sure that you have a good working knowledge of the ways brands are valued, so that you can apply that knowledge to a specific brand. In particular, you need to think about how the different methods relate to each other, and how using different methods will give different values. Keep up with the top ten brands, understanding the reasons for their strength

AUDITING MARKETING ACTIVITIES

LEARNING OUTCOMES

This unit has a very tight remit, focusing on audit of marketing activities. It

➡ Allows you to understand the process in conducting a detailed audit of an organization's marketing activities

➡ Develop your understanding of the potential measures of marketing performance

Techniques to be covered should include:

■ Balanced scorecard, with an emphasis on customer and innovation measures

■ Evaluation of marketing performance including the audit of marketing activities and valuation of marketing assets, such as brands

■ Financial techniques such as, shareholder value analysis (using total shareholder return and economic profit), financial ratio analysis, trend analysis, benchmarking and evaluation of historical financial decisions

Audit of marketing activities

One approach to assessing the overall marketing performance of the organization is to examine each element of the marketing mix in turn.

The 4Ps framework

(Product, Price, Place, Promotion), 5Ps (add People) or 7Ps (add Process and Physical Evidence).

The 4Ps-mix is generally the most accepted. It is often useful to set up a comparator, so that there is a measure of how customers perceive an offering (marketing mix) relative to a comparator.

This can be achieved by undertaking independent market research to identify and define the ideal expectations of customer needs in the desired market, and to set up the measures of what the customers would define as being well-satisfying, moderately satisfying and not satisfying.

An audit can be set up using each aspect of the marketing mix with a list of factors with clear definitions of what the customers expect from an ideal product.

There is a need to review historic performance as well as current. This concept is represented by Ohmae's strategic triangle (Figure 4.1):

The strategic triangle – 98 three Cs

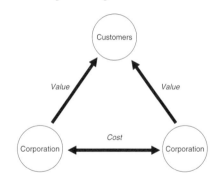

Source: Ohmae, K. (1982) The Mind of the Strategist

Ohmae (1982) states that in the construction of any business strategy, three main players must be taken into account, the corporation, the customer, and the competitor.

- The job of a marketing strategist is to achieve superior performance relative to the competiton, at the same time of ensuring that the strategy matches the key strengths of the organization, with the key needs of the marketplace

- Positive matching of the needs and objectives of both parties is essential for long-lasting relationships, without which the long-term viability of the firm in terms of shareholder value may be at stake

Ideal Marketing Mix Profile

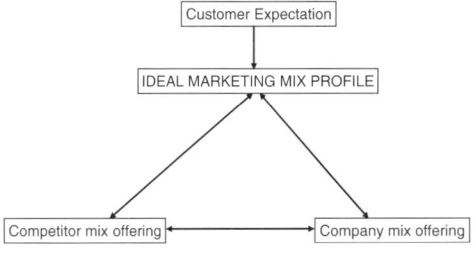

Fig. 4.1. Adapted strategic triangle – three Cs
Source: Ohmae, K. (1982) The Mind of the Strategist, McGraw Hill, Inc, 91 pp.

The actual audit will then be a checklist with a scoring system developed for a particular company competing in a specific industry setting.

It is useful to see competition as being on a number of levels.

Primary (or real)

Secondary (or peripheral)

■ Primary competition is – brands that are most similar. One of the easiest ways to assess which these brands are is to think about which brands the consumer would buy if your brand was not available. Or ideally, ask a sample of your target market that question

■ Secondary competitors are brands that are more distant from your own positioning. For example, a Cartier watch might be primary competition to Rolex. However, Rolex might view Swatch as secondary (or even tertiary) competition. Much depends on the need being met

Customer satisfaction and service quality

■ Another measure of product performance is the level of customer satisfaction. Satisfaction can be viewed as the difference between expectation and performance

■ Generally speaking, customer satisfaction is viewed as a short-term, transaction-specific measure, whereas service quality is an attitude formed by a long-term overall evaluation of a performance

Diagnosing service quality failure

The service quality process can be described in terms of the gaps between customer expectation and perceptions on the part of management, employees, and customers. The most important gap is between customers' expectation of service and their perception of the service actually delivered. The goal of the service company is to close that gap or at least narrow it as far as possible. Before that, four other gaps need to be closed or narrowed

Gap 1 – Difference between what the consumers expect of a service and what management perceives consumers expect

Gap 2 – Difference between what management perceives consumers expect and the quality specifications set for service delivery

Gap 3 – Difference between the quality specifications set for service delivery and the actual quality of service delivery

Gap 4 – Difference between the actual quality of service delivery and the quality of service delivery described in the firm's external communications.

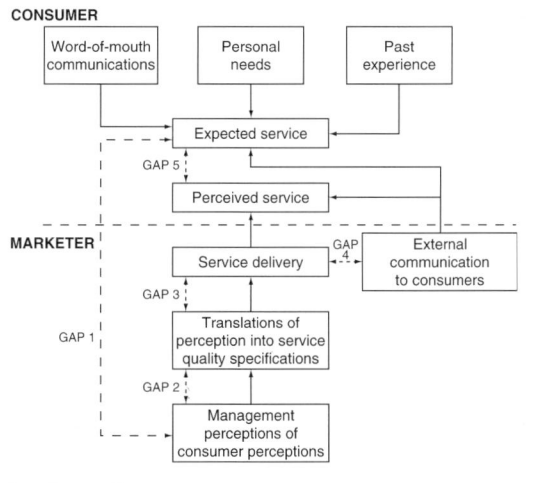

Fig. 4.2. Conceptual model of service quality
Source: Berry, Parasuraman and Zeithaml (1994)

SERVQUAL

One well-accepted research instrument used to assess service quality is a questionnaire called SERVQUAL. It sees service quality as the gap between performance and expectations in the same way as customer satisfaction might be measured. The questionnaire is a 44-item scale which measures customer expectations and perceptions with regard to five quality dimensions.

It compares consumer perception of service quality of an organization against the consumer expectation of an excellent company in the same category.

The whole organization must be focused on the task. Processes need to be analysed and evaluated to check – what happens if it goes wrong?

Dimension	Description	E/P	Example item
Tangibles	Tangible evidence, e.g., carpeting, lighting, brochures, correspondence, appearance of personnel	Expectation	Employees of excellent companies will be neat in appearance
		Perception	ABC's employees are neat in appearance
Reliability	The same level of service each time, e.g., accurate invoicing, accurate records	Expectation	When excellent companies promise to do something by a certain time, they will do so
		Perception	When ABC promise to do something by a certain time, they will do so
Responsiveness	Commitment to provide services in a timely manner, e.g., willingness, readiness, preparedness of employees	Expectation	Employees of excellent companies give prompt service to customers
		Perception	Employees of ABC give prompt service to customers

Fig. 4.3. The five quality dimensions of SERVQUAL

Dimension	Description	E/P	Example item
Assurance	The competence of the firm, the courtesy to its customers, the security of operations, e.g. has required skills to perform the service	Expectation	Customers of excellent companies will feel safe in their transactions
		Perception	Customers of ABC will feel safe in their transactions
Empathy	Ability to experience another's feeling as one's own, e.g., understand customer needs and respond to them, are accessible	Expectation	Excellent companies will give customers individual attention
		Perception	ABC gives you individual attention

Fig. 4.3. Continued
Source: Adapted from Parasuraman, Berry and Zeithaml (1991)

Complaining

Many customers seem reluctant to complain. This creates problems for marketers.

1. Dissatisfied customers may stop buying. Repeat purchase will be reduced

2. Dissatisfied customers will pass on negative comments discouraging other potential buyers

3. The level of complaints is likely to underestimate the actual level of underlying dissatisfaction

4. Cross selling is likely to be reduced

5. Latent dissatisfaction means that the competitive threat may be underestimated

6. An opportunity is missed for service recovery. Companies need to set up an efficient complaints handling process

Price

To assess the effectiveness of the price element of the mix, the following information is needed:

1. The pricing strategy

2. Costs

3. Competitor pricing

Pricing strategy

There is a need to understand the aims of the pricing strategy before assessing whether it is the right one.

■ Is the aim market penetration or market skimming?

■ Is the profit target survival or optimisation? What does a price suggest about quality?

■ A pricing strategy needs to take into account three factors, demand, cost and competition

Costs

- One of price's main contributions to the marketing mix is its effect on profit as profit is essentially the difference between revenue (i.e., price–volume) and cost. It also affects profit via the mechanism of price elasticity. Price elasticity is specific to product categories and varies over time

- It is not always as simple as saying spend more on the profitable lines and get rid of the unprofitable ones. There are a number of other factors to take into account

- Strategic implications – Lines may be there for reasons other than simply profit. They may fulfil a strategic purpose such as acting as loss leaders to gain entry to a retailer, or to act as complements to other more profitable lines so that a complete range may be offered

- Sharing of overheads – By removing unprofitable lines, the fixed costs will be shared between fewer lines hence affecting the profitability of the remaining lines

- Impact on relative marketing overhead – If more is spent on the more profitable lines, then a greater proportion of the marketing overheads should be allocated to these lines, with the result that they become less profitable, so we should be spending less on them

Assessing price competitiveness

In virtually every market, there are competitors. The relative price/quality position in the marketplace needs to be understood. This involves developing a specific positioning map based on value. To do this, the quality and price of each competitor needs to be measured. This can be done in a number of ways. Ideally, a lot of customer data would be collected.

Customer data

1. The dimensions of quality that matter to them, i.e., what and how important are the attributes on which they are assessing competitive offerings?

2. How do our products and our competitors rate on each of these attributes?

3. What are their perceptions of price?

4. What price/quality combinations are most valued by customers?

Promotion

■ The promotional mix can be divided into its separate elements and analysed separately or amalgamated and viewed holistically

■ We need to determine firstly what we are trying to achieve. For a sales promotion it may be an upturn in sales, for advertising it may be an increase in awareness, for public relations it may be an improved brand image or front-of-mind saliency

■ The next stage is to determine which measures are appropriate. The same measures for each or alter them according to the characteristics of the element of the mix

Target audience	Objectives	Measures
Manufacturer to intermediary	Stimulate intermediaries to try new products	Listings
	Encourage intermediaries to increase shelf space for existing product	Retail audits
Intermediaries to consumers	Generate higher levels of store traffic	Footfall
Manufacturers to consumers	Encourage consumer trial	Consumer market research on trial, frequency, weight
	Increase frequency of purchase	
	Increase weight of purchase	Possible use of panel data
Manufacturers to sales force	Build performance	Performance against targets and historic sales

Fig. 4.4. Examples of sales promotion evaluation

Measure definition

- Expenditure – Amount spent on advertising
- Share of voice – Relative spend compared to competitors within sector (called share of outlays in the USA)
- Exposure – No. of times an ad is delivered to a consumer
- Reach – No. of households exposed at least once to an ad in a given time period
- Rating – % of the population viewing an ad in a given time period
- Frequency – No. of exposures of an ad in a given time period
- GRPs – Gross rating points are the sum of all ratings
- Trial First purchase of brand
- Average frequency is the average number of exposures delivered in a period, calculated by dividing GRPs by the average reach of a campaign

Stage in communication	Type of variable	Typical measures
Firm's advertising input	Intensity	Spend, relative spend, exposures, rating, reach, frequency, gross rating points, share of voice
	Media	TV, radio, newspapers, magazines, telephone, internet, outdoor, mail, classified directories
	Ad content: Creative	Argument and other verbal cues; pictures, sound and other emotional cues; endorsement and other inferential cues
Consumer's mental processes	Cognitive	Thoughts, recognition, recall (prompted and spontaneous)
	Affective	Warmth, liking, attitude
	Conative	Persuasion, purchase intention
Market outcomes	Brand choice	Trial, repurchase, switching
	Purchase intensity	Incidence, frequency, weight
	Financial	Market share, revenue, profits

Fig. 4.5. Model and measures of advertising effectiveness
Source: Adapted from Tellis (2004, p. 44)

Place – Distribution

Distribution lacks the visibility and glamour of, say, promotion but is still a vital part of an effective marketing mix. According to Rosenbloom (1999), the most widely used performance criteria for channel members are:

1. Sales performance
2. Inventory maintenance
3. Selling capabilities
4. Competitive products handled
5. Growth prospects.

To this, might be added:

1. Profitability and
2. Strategic fit.

Hints and tips

■ Examiners are interested in your ability to see the strategic implications of your analysis. Whenever you conduct a piece of analysis, think what it means. Ask yourself the question 'So what?'

■ Exam questions are likely to ask you to consider a number marketing activities related to an industry or organizational example, and you will need to be able to take a theoretical framework such as the 4Ps, Value Chain or the 7S framework

EVALUATING PERFORMANCE: FINANCIAL MEASURES

Unit 5

LEARNING OUTCOMES

➡ The purpose of this unit is to enable you to understand the importance of financial measures in the strategic decision-making process (without making you into an accountant!). The emphasis is on helping you to understand the range of measures available and their contribution in helping you to reach a decision. In an examination you might be expected to calculate a few of the more basic ratios, at most. What is more important, however, is that you understand what they mean and what conclusions they can help you to reach

In this unit you will:

■ Understand the quantitative techniques which can be used to evaluate business performance

■ Examine financial measures

■ Explain the purpose and contribution of financial evaluation of performance of strategic analysis

■ Use the various financial measures of performance appropriately

■ Use financial ratio analysis, benchmarking, shareholder value analysis and trend analysis

■ Evaluate performance over current and historic business cycles

■ Understanding competitive financial strength and weaknesses is imperative

KEY DEFINITIONS

Assets are resources that the organization owns and will provide a future benefit to the business

Fixed assets are held and used over a long period of time (e.g., land, buildings, plant, and equipment)

Current assets are owned for just a short period (e.g., stocks and cash)

Stock (in the US, inventory) is the goods purchased for resale or manufacture (e.g., raw materials, work-in-progress or finished goods)

Debtors (in the US, accounts receivable) are both the people to whom the company owes money and the money owed to them

Liabilities represent the amount the company owes its creditors

Creditors (in the US, accounts payable) are the people who owe money to the company and the money it owes to them

Capital is the part of the fund of the business provided by its owners

Cost of sales are operating expenses not treated as distribution costs or administrative expenses

Net operating profit is operating profit minus taxes

Capital employed is the sum of shareholders' funds, creditors (over a year), and provision for liabilities and charges

- Porter (1985). The value chain is a means of helping to understand all the activities involved within the organization (value chain) as well as outside organization (the value system)

- Having access to information regarding a competitor's cost structure and how they can finance these costs can provide a significant insight into how competitors are delivering value. This would help with the positioning of a company relative to others

- An additional framework developed by Hamel and Prahalad is similar to Porter's Value Chain (1985) and shows a better representation of where financial appraisal sits within the strategy formulation process.

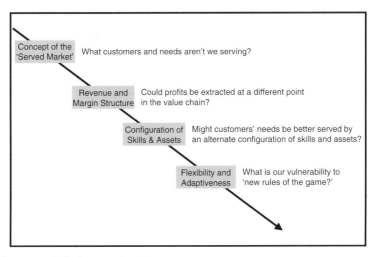

Fig. 5.1. Interpreting an organization's economic engine
Source: Hamel and Prahalad (1994)

- This model uses the analogy of an engine to represent the organization and integrate marketing, finance, and operations functions to provide a framework that can drill into the different parts of the organization in order to be able to provide an overall strategic competence level of the organization

- Financial measures are often used as control mechanisms to check whether strategies have worked. It is important to bear in mind that many marketing activities such as advertising and PR have a delayed effect, and therefore just because sales and profits are not immediately realised, it does not mean that the campaign is not working

- Within marketing, the most important application of finance is probably pricing, where financial data, particularly cost data is used by companies to set prices. Pricing is possibly the most important component of the marketing mix, as it sets the precedence for all other parts of the mix

Financial statements

- Financial statements, such as the balance sheet and the profit and loss account, provide historical information, not current or future information. But history can be useful as an indicator of the future

- A profit and loss account presents information about an organization's financial performance throughout a period; a balance sheet gives information about its financial position at a certain point in time, i.e., the balance sheet date

Profit

- The obvious definition of profit is the excess of revenue (or sales turnover) in a period, over costs and other expenditure in the same period

- However, financial statements tend to view profit on a number of levels and it is important to understand at which level profit is being calculated in your organization to make both historic and competitor comparisons

- Gross profit, for example, is sales turnover minus cost of sales

- Net profit (or operating profit) is gross profit minus distribution and administrative costs

Costs

- It is important to understand how costs are allocated within your organization. There are many different types of cost, and organizations may treat them differently. This can all get very complicated, but all we are going to cover here are the basics of fixed and variable costs

- Essentially, a 'fixed cost' (sometimes called an overhead) is one which will remain the same for a given period of time (i.e., will be a fixed amount) regardless of the volume of activity in the period

■ These costs increase over time, but are fixed for a given period of time. The important point is that the cost per period, such as the cost per month, does not vary with the amount of activity

Using financial ratio analysis

■ Ratios can be used very effectively in the analysis stage

■ Trends by comparing a firm's performance over time

■ Benchmarking against the competition since performance with others can be compared

■ When making comparisons between firms, there is a need to decide which type of business is comparable. There is a need to find a business with a similar trading pattern. The following factors might be considered: type of industry, nationality, regional area, and size of business

Broadly speaking, there are five different types of ratio:

1. Profitability ratios (including return on investment)
2. Asset utilization ratios
3. Liquidity ratios
4. Capital structure ratios
5. Investor ratios

Profitability ratios

The main measures of profit used therefore are return on capital or return on investment.

Return on Capital Employed (ROCE)

The total capital employed in a company can be measured in several ways, but these should all give the same figure.

1. Fixed assets plus net current assets
2. Current assets minus current liabilities
3. Share capital plus reserves plus long-term creditors and provisions for liabilities and charges

Asset utilization ratios

This set of ratios looks at the use of resources by the organization.

■ Stock turnover – The rate at which a business converts its stock into sales is a critical indicator of business activity. The stock turnover ratio tells us the number of times the stock is completely sold and replaced by purchases during the accounting period. But remember the trading cycle may be cyclical, resulting in peak and low stock levels, so the timing of this measure may be crucial

■ Average debtor collection period – This ratio estimates the number of days of sales, which are represented by the firm's debtors

■ Ratio of asset values to sales – This ratio looks at the ability of the assets employed by the company to generate sales revenue. It is calculated by dividing the sales revenue by the total asset base (the sum of fixed assets and current assets). This ratio gives an indication of the ability of the assets to generate profit

Liquidity ratios

■ Liquidity ratios are used to assess whether the organization has enough cash to meet the payments due for its current liabilities. This is called short-term solvency

■ Current ratio – This is the standard test of liquidity and is the ratio of current assets to current liabilities

■ A ratio above 1.0 would normally be expected, but this varies from industry to industry. Any organization with a ratio of below 1.0 faces a risk of not being able to pay its debts on time. An acceptable current ratio is 1.5, but this is only a rough guide, depending on the industry

■ Most analysts would be concerned if a manufacturing firm's current ratio falls below 2:1, but a lower ratio would be acceptable in firms with little or no stock

The assumption with the current ratio is that the organization is able to convert all its current assets into cash relatively easily.

■ The acid test ratio – The acid test ratio, or quick ratio as it is sometimes known, takes account of the illiquidity of some assets. It removes stocks from the calculation allowing for a fairer assessment of the liquidity of some companies

■ This ratio should be at least 1.0 for companies with low stock turnover. For those with a high stock turnover, this ratio can be lower than 1.0 without suggesting that the company has cash flow problems. An acceptable quick ratio may be 0.8, but again this is dependent on the industry, and is just a rough guide

- Whilst a low liquidity ratio tends to be bad, a high liquidity ratio is not always good. The company may be tying up more money in the business than it needs to be

- The trend in liquidity ratios should also be monitored, whether the organization chooses to use the current ratio or quick ratio, or both. Changes in the ratio can show if the company's solvency position is improving or declining

Capital structure ratios

- The main ratio is the gearing ratio. Gearing is a UK term; the US equivalent is leverage. In highly geared companies, a small change in the operating profits will result in a much larger percentage change in earnings per share than in a lower geared company

- An analysis of the financial structure of the company is important to both the owners and creditors. It is important because the amount of debt increases the sensitivity of variation in profit. Investment in a highly geared company carries more risk of low returns, but also more possibility of high returns. A ratio of more than 0.5 would show that lenders, are contributing more capital than the owners. For the lenders, this would generally be unacceptable.

Investor ratios

- Various ratios are used by investors and investment analysts to assess the value and performance of equity investments. Some of these are obtained from, or at least partially derived from financial statements

■ Earnings per share (EPS) – This is the amount of profit earned by the company during a financial year that can be attributed to each ordinary share.This is often used by investors as a measure of corporate performance, and can be used to assess corporate trends over time

■ Price to earnings ratio (P/E ratio) – Another commonly used investment ratio, the P/E ratio, expresses the share price as a multiple of the EPS. A high P/E ratio indicates strong investor confidence

■ Dividends per share – Very few, if any, companies retain their profits for internal investment – it is only dividends which the owners of shares receive

■ Dividend cover – The dividend cover is the number of times the annual dividend is covered by earnings

Limitations of ratio analysis

■ Ratios are valuable, but need to be used with caution. The calculation of ratios is objective and accurate, but that does not mean that financial analysis is similarly objective

■ The two-year problem – Comparing only two years where one may be atypical, i.e., especially good or especially bad and unlikely to be repeated

■ The snapshot problem – Using figures from a balance sheet will only tell you what the situation was on one particular day

■ The apples and pears problem – No two companies are the same even if they operate in the same industry

■ The history problem – Ratios are invariably calculated from past data

- Ratios are largely subjective and their analysis still remains more of an art than a science
- Ratio analysis is only an analysis of the financial affairs of a company. It cannot analyse non-financial matters such as improving customer relations, potential labour difficulties, etc.

Shareholder value analysis

Shareholder value analysis has evolved as a result of the shortcomings of other valuation techniques. Shareholder Value is a long-term measure. It also gives a better view of the future as it is less susceptible to short-term blips

Asset-based valuations, for example, have limitations. They:

- Do not take account the future potential use of those assets

- Use subjective assumptions
- Are often only useful if the business is going to be cannibalized and the individual assets sold off on a piecemeal basis. If the business is being taken over as a going concern, the intangible assets are likely to be underestimated

Profit-based valuations are limited. They:

- Are less useful in assessing future potential cash flows
- The multiplier used for profit is subjective
- Major companies have adopted this approach to place value on firms to be divested and acquired, and also to evaluate business units and their strategic options within the company. SVA can be used directly to evaluate a business or strategy

Economic value added (analysis)

Economic value added (EVA) goes beyond shareholder value analysis by adding in the idea that every business employs capital in some way. That capital may be plant, stock, working capital, etc. It doesn't matter what sort of capital it is, but the important issue is that it comes with a cost. EVA builds on SVA by adding the additional variable of cost of capital into the mix

- Essentially EVA uses an SVA perspective to evaluate business performance taking into account profits, cost of capital and capital employed.

- One technique is to imagine shareholder value as a tube of future cash flows. The cylinder needs to be as long, as wide and as fast flowing as possible. The greater the volume contained in the tube, the more the shareholder value

ANALYSING THE EXTERNAL ENVIRONMENT

Unit 6

There are external factors beyond every organization's control to which they must respond. The first stage to determining how to respond to these is to understand what these forces are, and how significant they are to your organization

LEARNING OUTCOMES

In this unit you will:

➡ Appreciate the difference between the macro- and micro-environment

➡ Evaluate the techniques available to allow the objective assessment of the external environment including frameworks such as PEST and Porter's Five Forces

➡ Understand the tools used to evaluate an organization's competitive position

➡ Study the means of analysing potential and current customer bases to gain understanding

Having completed this unit you will be able to:

➡ Define the organization's intelligence/research/resource needs to support a rigorous environmental audit

➡ Undertake customer and competitor analyses at the micro level

➡ Assess the political, economic, and social, and technological trends at the macro level

➡ Assess the organization's competitive position in relation to them

➡ Draw together the results of the internal and external analyses to give a summary of the organization's competitive position

KEY DEFINITIONS

Marketing environment is the set of uncontrollable external forces to which a company must adapt

The macro-environment consists of macro-factors and their trends such as politics, economics, societal and technological developments on a national and, if relevant to the business, a global scale

The micro-environment consists of trends at the industry level such as suppliers, competitors, and customers

Environmental scanning is the process of monitoring the environment, and gathering relevant market intelligence to ensure that the organization remains up to date with trends

The marketing environment constitutes the arena in which the organizations go about their business

Environmental monitoring

Environmental monitoring in an organization is often a marketing responsibility. It consists of the following steps:

- Selection of the driving forces, or drivers, that are most likely to have an impact on the organization's activities
- Key drivers are usually selected for particular attention as it is not possible to monitor all factors closely
- Collection of information on these factors
- Evaluation of information and forecasting of likely environmental changes
- Assessment of how the changes will affect the organization
- Adjustment of marketing strategy and mix to minimize the negative and maximize the positive impact

Scanning

This can take three forms:

- Continuous – Companies should monitor their main stakeholders, customers, and competitors to identify changes and trends
- Periodic – It makes sense for organizations to undertake periodic research, e.g., at the beginning of a planning cycle
- Irregular or ad hoc – Tailored research may be undertaken for a specific project,
- Changes in the environment may be either continuous or discontinuous
- Continuous changes are called trends and may be either fast or slow. Discontinuous changes are one-off events or environmental shocks and are by their nature, hard to predict

The macro- and micro-environments

The marketing environment (Figure 6.1) is divided into two areas:

1. The 'macro-environment' consisting of those factors furthest from the organization, which it can neither control nor influence

2. The 'micro-environment' consisting of those factors close to an organization which, although it cannot control them directly, may be able to influence indirectly through marketing campaigns

Fig. 6.1. An overview of the marketing environment

The macro-environment

The macro-environment includes the following:

- Demographic factors
- Economic factors
- Social and cultural factors
- Legal and political factors
- Physical factors
- Technological factors

This is a PEST analysis – an acronym for Political, Economic, Social and Technological factors.

The micro-environment

The micro environment includes the following factors:

- Customers
- Competition
- Suppliers
- Intermediaries
- Publics
- The organization itself

Customers

An organization's customers form a key component of its micro-environment. These include direct customers and more indirect consumers further down the distribution chain.

Monitoring questions include:

- Who are our customers?
- How many of them are there?
- Is that number growing or declining?
- Is the customer base static or changing?
- What do they want?
- Who, apart from us, do they deal with?

Competition

Identifying competitors is a crucial task within marketing, but it is not always as easy as it may seem. We need to know what competes for customers' interest, time, and money – directly and indirectly

Porter identified four components of competitor analysis:

1. Future goals
2. Assumptions
3. Current strategy
4. Capabilities

■ As strategic analysis is concerned essentially with the future – where are competitors are going. What are their aims geographically, in products and markets?

■ Assumptions underlie strategies and action. Often they are implicit, but from various sources, it may be possible to find out how the competitor thinks about the industry. What do they think are the major drivers?

■ Their current strategy should at least be clear – at least insofar as they have an explicit strategy. Although it is decreasingly common, many firms do not seem to have thought through what they are doing and why, they merely carry on as before and react to events

■ Capabilities we also probably have a good idea about, but it is helpful to take a more formal approach. A SWOT analysis applied to the major competitors is a simple initial approach. A more quantitative method is to take the critical success factors (CSFs, or key success factors, KSFs) and rate ourselves and the competitors on each. An example is shown in Figure 6.2

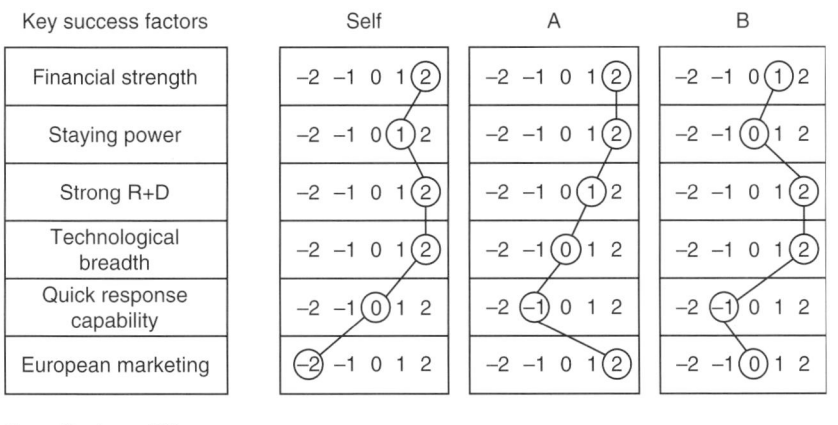

Fig. 6.2. Competitors' capabilities
Source: Hooley and Saunders (1993, p. 125)

- The more difficult task is to forecast future capabilities, particularly of new competitors. This can only be done through a careful analysis of their current competencies and resources, together with a view of their future goals

- Suppliers are important in ensuring a steady flow of products from the producer to the end-user. They can also be a source of new developments and information about the marketplace

- Publics – A public is any group which has an interest in an organization and its activities, and which has a potential impact on the organization's ability to achieve its objectives

Porter's five forces

Porter's model of the forces that interact to produce the competitive situation in an industry is one of the most famous in business literature. It is reproduced as Figure 6.3. Porter identifies the five forces as:

1. Threat of new entrants
2. Bargaining power of suppliers
3. Bargaining power of buyers
4. Threat of substitutes
5. Intensity of rivalry

Porter gives detailed suggestions for analysing each of these.

Fig. 6.3. Porter's five forces
Source: Porter (1985)

Entry barriers

Economies of scale
Proprietary product differences
Brand identity
Switching costs
Capital requirements
Access to distribution
Absolute cost advantages
Proprietary learning curve
Access to necessary inputs
Government policy
Expected retaliation

Determinants of supplier power

Differentiation of inputs
Switching cost of suppliers and firms in the industry
Presence of substitute inputs
Supplier concentration
Importance of volume to supplier
Cost relative to total purchases in the industry
Impact of inputs on cost or differentiation
Threat of forward integration relative to threat of backward integration by firms in the industry

Rivalry determinants

Industry growth
Fixed (or storage) costs/value added
Intermittent overcapacity
Product differences
Brand identity
Switching costs
Concentration and balance
Informational complexity
Diversity of competitors
Corporate stakes
Exit barriers

Determinants of substitution threat

Relative price performance of substitutes
Switching costs
Buyer propensity to substitute

Determinants of buyer power Bargaining leverage

Buyer concentration versus firm concentration
Buyer volume
Buyer switching costs relative to firm switching costs
Buyer information
Ability to backward integrate
Substitute products
Pull-through

Price sensitivity

Price/total purchases
Product differences
Brand identity
Impact on quality/performance
Buyer profits
Decision makers' incentives

Consolidating the analysis

There are several frameworks we can use. These are not mutually exclusive and may be usefully combined to pull out key themes.

1. SWOT analysis – This well-known framework can be used to distill the analysis and summarize the outcomes of the internal analysis into strengths and weaknesses, and the external analysis into opportunities and threats

2. Issue analysis – This is a broader-based approach and avoids some of the problems inherent in the classification required by the SWOT analysis

3. The 6Cs framework

The issue analysis approach described above is a very open-ended approach. A possible framework is that of the 6Cs.

These are:

■ Customers and the market

■ Competitive position

■ Core competencies and assets

■ Chances and opportunities

■ Critical success factors (CSFs) or problems to be overcome

■ Constraints

Process of strategic audit

We start with little knowledge, gather lots of data and refine it, ending with a summary of the issues which are important (Figure 6.4).

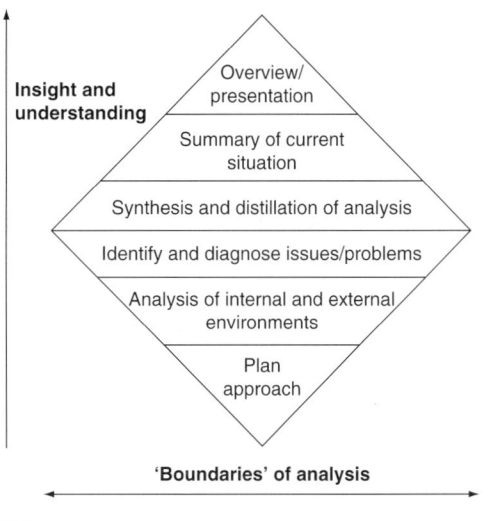

Fig. 6.4. Process of strategic audit

ANALYSING THE INTERNAL ENVIRONMENT

LEARNING OBJECTIVES

➡ Having analysed the external environment and its implication for the organization an internal audit of the firm's current resources, competencies and capabilities is needed to identify whether it has the appropriate ones to serve its current customers, as well as identifying whether it has the right set of competencies to serve its customers in the future

➡ Several techniques are available to an organization in order to assess its capabilities of how it delivers value and you should be able to apply these techniques to any organizational setting to determine this

KEY DEFINITIONS

The internal environment is the set of factors within the organization which affects its success within the marketplace

Portfolio analysis involves assessing the relative attractiveness of products within the range (or businesses within the company) to allow for informed decisions on resource allocation

Value chain analysis divides organizational activities into five core activities and four supporting activities, which allows for a detailed evaluation of how value is added

Resource-based view (RBV) suggests that high performance depends on historic resources

Models to assess attractiveness of products and markets

Portfolio analysis models

■ Two of the more commonly found models are described here – the Boston box and the directional policy matrix

■ Portfolio models provide managers with a clear framework within which to make their decisions

■ All portfolio models involve a classification and display of the current and potential positions of businesses and products according to the attractiveness of that market and the ability of the business to compete within that market

BCG growth–share matrix

The two principal factors with which the BCG grid is concerned are:

■ Market share
■ Market growth

Market share

To understand the importance of market share, you need to understand the impact of the learning curve (Figure 7.2), which suggests that the more often we perform a certain activity, the more efficient we get at doing it. This is for several reasons:

■ Labour efficiency – Those actually performing the function understand what they are supposed to be doing and perform it more effectively as they become more experienced

- Work specialization – As the volumes increase, companies can afford to specialize units of work into smaller units

- Methods improvement – The more often a company has to produce a particular product, the more likely it is to find a better (quicker and cheaper) way of doing it

- Economies of scale – As the company produces more, the costs of raw materials and so on should go down

- The Boston Consultancy Group wanted to quantify this learning curve effect, to give some idea of the cost advantage a company producing more would have over one producing less. Its work suggested that a decline of up to 30 per cent in costs would occur for each cumulative doubling of output

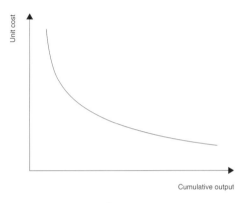

Fig. 7.1. Learning curve effect

Market growth

- Market growth is a measure of the attractiveness of the market
- Products move through a series of stages each with its own characteristics
- They begin life in the introductory phase – relatively slow sales growth and very low sales
- The growth rate then increases dramatically as the product begins to recoup its development costs and move into profit
- After a period of time (and this can almost literally be of any length), sales will start to flatten out as the market becomes saturated and enters the mature phase
- Eventually, the product's sales will start to decline as new products take its place

We shall now examine the characteristics of products lying within the different quadrants.

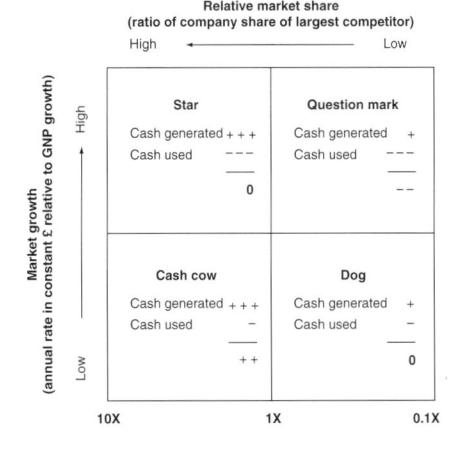

Fig. 7.2. Growth–share matrix
Source: Boston Consultancy Group

Cash cows

■ Cash cows have dominant positions in slow or no-growth markets, that is markets in their mature phase. They are profitable and cash positive. They need some investment as their position of dominance must be maintained, but the excess cash can be siphoned-off to fund other categories

Stars

■ Stars also tend to be profitable because of their strong share position. They may be self-financing or may provide or require cash at the margins. However, the present cash needs will tend to be modest in scale and will be more than compensated for when the growth rate of the market slows. Then the product, provided that it has maintained its dominant position, will move into the cash cow category

Problem children

■ This category is also known as 'question marks' or 'wildcats'. They have a low relative market share, but operate in markets of rapid growth. It is costly just to maintain share, but an obvious objective for 'question marks' is to build share to a dominant position

Dogs

■ Dogs are products with a low share in a low- or no-growth market. They are best regarded as 'cash traps' as they are unlikely to ever generate cash themselves. As there can only be one leader in a market and most markets are mature, the greatest number of products and businesses fall into this sector

Strategic implications

■ Over time, products will move because of market dynamics and strategy decisions. The objective is to analyse the current portfolio matrix and understand the natural dynamics of the portfolio so that a strong portfolio will result in the future. Over time, all products would fall down the grid so that 'stars' become 'cash cows' and 'question marks' become 'dogs' – provided that the relative share position has been maintained

■ Some companies view investing in 'dogs' and 'cash cows' as 'safer', investing less than is needed in both 'question marks' and 'stars'

Strategic alternatives

The outline strategic alternatives for each of the quadrants in relation to marketing strategy are as follows:

■ Cash cows – use profits to maintain position and fund stars/question marks

■ Stars – maintain/increase share

■ Question marks – either intensify efforts, or maintain current strategy, or leave the market

■ Dogs – reduce efforts, maintain, or divest

Weaknesses in the BCG grid

The BCG grid is a very useful tool, but it needs to be used with caution. One of the main problems is how the measures are determined

Product-market definition

■ A business segment or product market is correctly defined if it is possible to establish and defend a competitive advantage in that segment alone, without the need to participate in other segments

Market share estimates

■ Whenever a market share is used to evaluate performance, managers become adept at moving the market boundaries to show a static or an increasing share. The resulting narrow view of the market may result in threats and opportunities being overlooked

Market growth rate

■ This can also be manipulated where wishful thinking may lead to a higher growth rate being predicted than is realistic

Relationship between share and profitability

■ The BCG grid assumes a direct causal relationship between market share and profitability. This is, to say the least, an oversimplification of the issue. It is important to remember that the learning curve effect relates only to relative profitability within the industry. It takes no account of the fact that some industries are inherently more profitable than others

Market share can be important, but other factors need to be considered in evaluating its role in profitability:

■ Size of business – In some industries, both niche and multinational companies prosper

■ Type of industry – Market share appears to be more important in high-tech industries. In the service sector, diseconomies of scale can occur leading to reduced profitability

■ Stage in the product life cycle – PIMS research has shown that profitability differentials narrow as the market matures. On average, a company with twice the share of its leading competitor (relative market share of 2.0) would have a direct cost advantage of 3.5 per cent in less mature markets and only 1.2 per cent in mature markets

■ Unionization – This appears to mitigate the effect of large market share by ensuring that a larger percentage of costs end up as wages

■ A third variable, such as quality of management or perceived quality of product, may influence both market share and profits. More recent reviews of the PIMS data suggest that the direct causal impact of market share may account for only 10 to 20 per cent of the relationship

■ Empirical evidence from Porter and others suggests that companies with a strong share of a tightly defined/niche market have high return on investment (ROI). In the PIMS study, which looked at total rather than served markets, such companies would have been defined as having low market share.

■ To counteract many of these criticisms, and to support planning process more effectively, new portfolio models have been developed

■ The BCG grid can be viewed as an oversimplification of the market and, as a result, multifactor models have been developed that can be adapted to a variety of industries

Directional Policy matrix (DPM)

- The most commonly used multifactor model is the one often referred to as the directional policy matrix. This very similar to the GE matrix. The sectors are determined by assessing the strength of the strategic business unit (SBU), product group, individual product or segment on the two composite factors of market attractiveness and competitive (business) position

- Market attractiveness reflects the difference in average long-run profit potential for all participants in the market. Competitive position evaluates the profitability of the business relative to the competition. Managers select the factors that they believe are important in determining market attractiveness and competitive position

- There are two complementary approaches to developing the lists of factors. One is to select from a standard checklist that has been developed from those factors that have historically determined (either industry or relative profitability). The other is to select a series of pairs of units (businesses) – an attractive, and an unattractive one (to the company). Factors are then derived from noting the important differences

Factors contributing to market attractiveness

The following factors contribute to market attractiveness:

- Market factors
- Size, volume and value
- Size of segments
- Growth rate
- Stage in market life cycle
- Diversity of market
- Price elasticity
- Bargaining power of buyers
- Seasonality of demand
- Economic and technological factors
- Investment required
- Nature of investment
- Industry capacity
- Level and maturing of technology
- Utilization
- Barriers to entry/exit
- Availability of raw materials

Competitive factors

- Types of competitor
- Structure of competition
- Substitutes
- Degree of differentiation

Environmental factors

- Legal/regulatory framework
- Social acceptance
- Unionization, etc.

Once we have decided which factors we are going to use, we need some method of consolidating them into a single composite score. The section below outlines an approach we could take.

Assessing market attractiveness

Figure 7.3 offers a simple example of how we might assess the attractiveness of a market.

Factor	Score	Weighting	Ranking
Market size	0.5	30	15
Market growth	0.5	20	10
Level of competition	0.0	20	0
Barriers to entry	1.0	15	15
Investment required	1.0	15	15
Total		100	55

Fig. 7.3. Assessing market attractiveness

Factors influencing the strength of competitive position

Market position

- Relative market share
- Rate of change of share
- Variability of share across segments
- Perceived differentiation of quality/price/service
- Breadth of product range
- Company image

Economic and technological position

- Relative cost position
- Capacity utilization
- Technological position
- Patented technology, product or process

Capabilities

- Management strength and depth
- Marketing strength
- Distribution system
- Labour relations
- Manufacturing efficiency

Once all the significant factors are agreed, the next stage is to weight each according to its relative importance – it would be very unusual if all were equally important. Problems can occur when factors are interrelated – relative market share and cost position, for example. A factor also may be very significant in one market and not in another, so weights may be ignored if it is felt that they do not add anything other than a spurious scientific objectivity

Assessing competitive position

The profile of a unit with regard to its competitive position could look something like Figure 7.4.

Once composite scores have been calculated on both dimensions, the present position of the unit can be plotted on the grid in Figure 7.5.

Factor	Score	Weighting	Ranking
Relative market share	0.75	40	30
Manufacturing efficiency	0.50	20	10
Relative cost position	0.50	20	10
Distribution strength	1.00	20	20
Total		100	70

Fig. 7.4. Competitive position profile

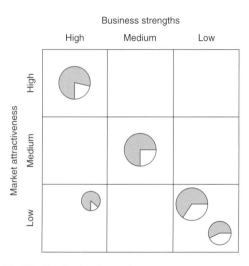

Business strengths

High   Medium   Low

Market attractiveness: High / Medium / Low

Fig. 7.5. Directional policy matrix

The figure illustrates an example of a completed DPM.

■ The SBUs/segments/brands which appear in the top left hand of the matrix are the stars

■ Those in the bottom left are the cash cows, which generate income for the organization

■ Those in the centre and top right are the equivalent of problem children, i.e., they have a question mark over their future. For these, a decision needs to be made to jump one way or another; either we decide to invest in them or we cut the losses

■ Products in the bottom right fall into the category of dogs and are unlikely to succeed. In most cases the best decision is to withdraw them or sell them to another company

Strategic implications

- Organizations need to review the performance of each of its SBUs, products or segments in the context of its overall mix. The relative position of each will help determine the appropriate strategy

- The organization has broadly a choice of four strategies. It may decide to:

- Build – increase the market share/develop further

- Maintain – stabilize current market share/use resource to maintain the status quo

- Harvest – sell off or pull off after milking the brand (or SBU, etc.) for its last potential profit

- Divest – drop or sell as soon as possible

Limitations of the multifactor model

- The multifactor model overcomes many of the criticisms of the BCG grid by adding greater complexity rather than relying on the simplicity of share and growth, but increased complexity leads to problems of its own. These are on two levels:

- The problem of having to reach a consensus on the factors and/or their weighting tends to bias results towards the 'medium' categories. Managers who disagree will compromise to reach a solution. The matrix will then lose its discriminatory power

- The use of composite scores can also mean that differences are lost in the process of generating a single score

Value chain analysis

Porter (1985) developed the concept of the value chain (Figure 7.6) which divides activities into five primary clusters, namely:

- Inbound logistics – how the company manages the flow of products into the company
- Operations – how the company changes the inputs into a saleable product, and adds value
- Outbound logistics – how the company distributes its product to its buyers
- Marketing and sales – activities that communicate to and motivate the buyers
- Service – the activities to keep the product working effectively for the buyer after purchase

These five primary activities are underpinned by four support activities.

- Procurement
- Human resource development
- Technological development
- Infrastructure

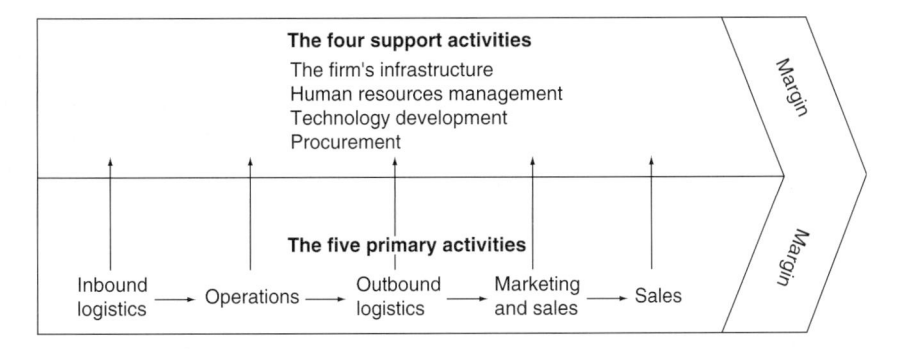

Fig. 7.6. The value chain
Source: Porter (1985)

The innovation audit

Successful companies innovate. They may innovate to create new products and services or be innovative in the way they operate, creating efficiencies within the value chain. The innovation audit provides a framework to uncover whether the necessary assets and competencies are available. It is divided into four main areas:

1. The current organizational climate and its impact on creativity

2. Measures of current performance in innovation

3. Policies and practices used to support innovation

4. Balance of the cognitive styles of the senior management team

Organizational climate

First, we need to conduct an attitude survey amongst staff to see how they feel about the organizational climate.

Attitude survey

The survey looked at how the employees view the organization's ability to support innovation and also to see what barriers exist to prevent staff from being creative (Figure 7.7).

Burnside (1990) lists 12 factors which are important in determining the level of innovation within a company. Eight of these are supportive of innovation and the remaining four are potential constraints.

Support		Constraint	
Factor	Description	Factor	Description
Teamwork	Level of commitment, level of trust, willingness to help each other	Time	Lack of time to consider alternative approaches to work
Resources	Access to resources such as facilities, staff, finance, etc.	Status quo	Traditional approach, unwillingness to change
Challenge	Challenge in work. Is it enough?	Politics	Territorial battles within the organization
Freedom	Amount of individual autonomy	Evaluation	Focus on criticism and external evaluation
Supervisor	Management support in goal setting, clear communication and morale		
Infrastructure	Level of senior management support and structures necessary for creativity		
Recognition	Level of recognition of and rewards for creativity		
Unity and co-operation	Collaborative and co-operative atmosphere, shared vision		

Fig. 7.7. Supporting and constraining factors on innovation

Cognitive styles of the senior management team

For the purpose of the innovation audit, we can look at four different cognitive styles and think about the impact these may have on the organization.

Cognitive style	Focuses on	Tends to be
Intuitive	Patterns, possibilities and ideas	Ingenious and integrative
Sensing	Here and now	Adaptable and practical
Thinking	Logic and objectivity	Pragmatic
Feeling	People and values	Empathetic

Fig. 7.8. Cognitive style

Hints and tips

■ Throughout this module, we stress the importance of using examples. But don't just quote ours – think of ones of your own. Originality will be rewarded in the examination

■ An important part of the module is in the application of theory in a particular context. Marks will be gained for applying the theory rather than just describing it

CHARACTERISTICS OF THE GLOBAL MARKETPLACE

Unit 8

KEY DEFINITIONS

Culture is patterned ways of thinking, feeling and reacting, acquired and transmitted mainly by symbols constituting the distinctive achievements of human groups including their embodiment in artefacts

Marketing Intelligence System is the systematic approach used to gather market intelligence

Porter (1986) divides the forces which drive international marketing into two: currents and cross-currents.

Figure 8.1 gives examples of these two types of force. Essentially, the currents are governed by macro forces, and the cross-currents by emergent trends.

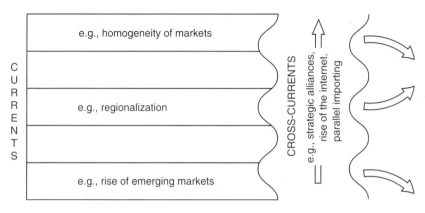

Fig. 8.1. Forces driving international marketing
Source: After Porter (1986)

Although international marketing is not conceptually different from domestic marketing, there are factors which may require additional attention.

1. Culture: markets can often be culturally diverse which can provide challenges particularly in the communications arena. Rules of business may differ

2. Markets: these can be geographically disparate leading to distribution and control problems

3. Data: market intelligence can be difficult and expensive to obtain, with problems of comparability

4. Politics: the relative stability of countries varies dramatically. Also the relative power of governments in regulating foreign trade vary

5. Economic: economies differ in levels of development, their finance systems, their regulatory bodies and the stability of their currency

International market intelligence gathering

The first stage in any market research programme is always to decide on the research objectives which need to be defined in terms of information requirements.

A basic list would be:

1. Where to go?
   - Assessment of global demand
   - Ranking of potential by country/region
   - Local competition
   - Political risk

2. How to get there?
   - Size of markets/segments
   - Barriers to entry
   - Transport and distribution costs
   - Local competition
   - Government requirements
   - Political risk
3. What shall we market?
   - Government regulations
   - Customer sophistication
   - Competitive stance

4. How do we persuade them to buy it?
   - Buyer behaviour
   - Competitive practice
   - Distribution channels
   - Promotional channel
   - Company expertise

Figure 8.2 adds to this basic list and shows how domestic firms need to adopt a structured approach to gathering international marketing intelligence.

The marketing environment	Differences across countries and regions of interest			Firm-specific historical data
	The competition	The product	Marketing mix	
Political context: leaders, national goals, ideology, key institution	Relative market shares, new product moves	Analysis of users. Who are the end-user industries?	Channels of distribution: evolution and performance	Sales trends by product and product-line, salesforce and customer
Economic growth prospects, business cycle stage	Pricing and cost structure, image and brand reputation	Industrial and consumer buyers; characteristics: size, age, sex, segment growth rates	Relative pricing elasticities and tactics	Trends by country and region
Per capita income levels, purchasing power	Quality: its attributes and positioning relative to competitors	Purchasing power and intentions	Advertising and promotion: choices and impacts on customers	Contribution margins

Fig. 8.2. The task of global marketing research: what should it determine?

The marketing environment	Differences across countries and regions of interest			Firm-specific historical data
	The competition	The product	Marketing mix	
End-user industry growth trends	Competitors' strengths: favourite tactics and Strategies	Customer response to new products, price, promotion	Service quality: perceptions and relative positioning	Marketing mix used, marketing response functions across countries and regions
Government: legislation, regulation, standards, barriers to trade		Switching behavior, role of credit and purchasing Future needs, impact of cultural differences	Logistics networks, configuration and change	

Fig. 8.2. Continued
Source: Terpstra and Sarathy (1997)

Secondary research

- International market research often begins with secondary data. There is generally a correlation between the stage of economic development and the availability, depth and accuracy of the information

- The internet is becoming the most popular tool for gathering secondary data with many useful websites easily available, often for free. The internet has revolutionized the ability of SMEs to carry out data searches. Another useful resource for UK companies is the Department of Trade and Industry (DTI) which provides a reasonably priced service based on a vast database and experienced staff

Primary research

Carter (2003) lists the following problems in conducting international market research.

- Costs – These vary with the UK being one of the cheapest and Japan one of the most expensive

- Language – In which language should the survey be conducted? Singapore with a population of 3 million has four official languages requiring four translations and four different ethnic interviewers

- Some concepts are very difficult to translate and may not have an exact parallel in another culture. Levels of literacy may be a problem

- Sample – Rural countries offer particular problems where respondents may be geographically scattered. There may be problems in interviewing female respondents in certain cultures

- Geography – Where do you conduct the study? Responses may differ widely depending on the product category

- Non-response – In some countries it may be hard to find respondents as interviewers are seen as akin to 'agents of the state'. Japanese respondents tend to be falsely positive in an attempt to please the interviewer

- Social organization – Family-owned businesses may value secrecy about their operations and may be unwilling to divulge information

- Terminology – This may differ from country to country. What do we mean by health food? Affluent? Middle age? Green?

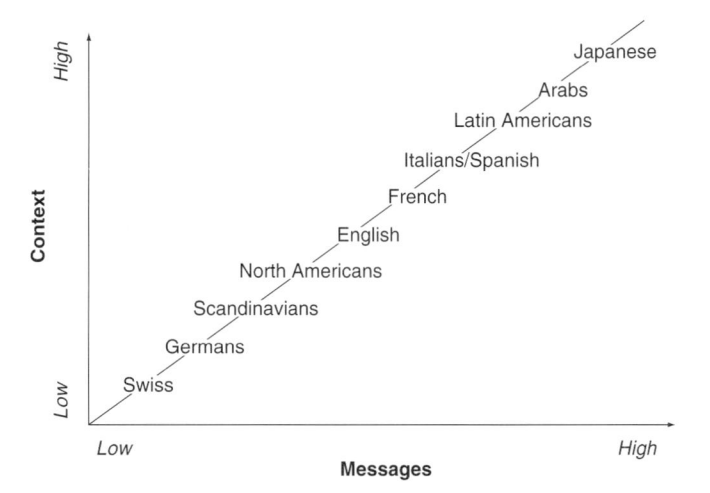

Fig. 8.3. The contextual continuum of differing cultures
Source: From Usunier, adapted from Edward T. Hall

A useful way to examine other cultures is to use Lee's Self Reference Criterion (SRC). This is a fourstep process designed to help organizations isolate essential cultural differences.

1. Look at the situation through the eyes of the home culture

2. Define the problem from step 1 through the eyes of the foreign culture

3. Find the gap between the cultures in steps 1 and 2 and how this will influence problem

4. Bridge the gap between the cultures

Scanning the international markets/countries.

The process of selecting an international target is often a multi-stage process as illustrated in the Figure 8.4.

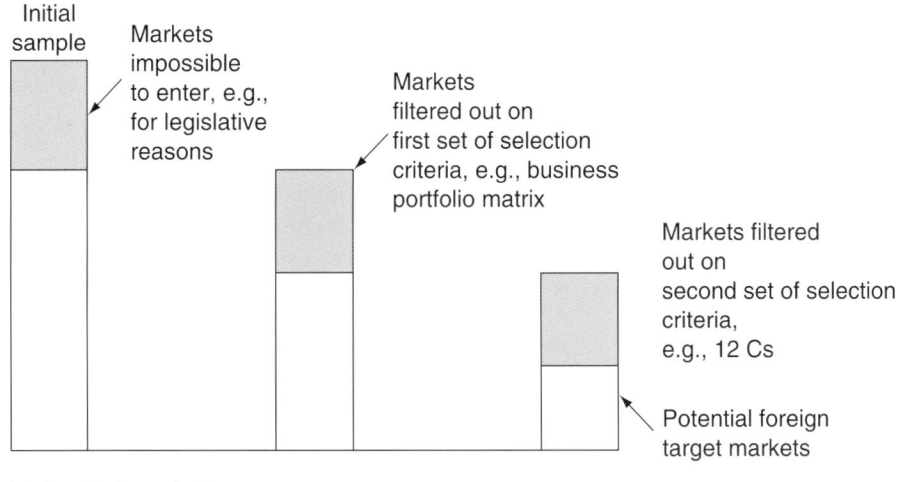

Fig. 8.4. A multi-stage selection process

In the initial stage of evaluating international markets, it makes sense to scan many countries but only relatively superficially.

Three useful criteria to use at this stage are:

1. Accessibility – Can we get there? What's preventing us? Trade barriers? Legislation? Geography?

2. Profitability – What percentage of the population can afford our product? What is the level of competitive activity? What's the exchange rate? What are the payment terms?

3. Market size – Present and future trends

- Having undertaken this initial scanning, the marketer will have developed a list of countries where marketing opportunities exist

- The next stage is to make an assessment of their viability. We can define three types of market opportunity

  - Existing markets – The market is already supplied by competitors. Market entry will be difficult unless the company has a superior product or new concept

  - Latent markets – Potential customers exist whose needs are not being met. No competition allowing for easier market entry

  - Incipient markets – Markets which may emerge in the future but do not exist at present

The nature of the product offered can be analysed in a similar way also categorizing in three ways:

■ Competitive product – Broadly similar to those already in the marketplace

■ Improved product – A product which offers some improvement on existing products available but is not unique

■ Breakthrough product – An innovation offering a significant competitive advantage

We can pull these two sets of factors together to give a matrix of product/market combinations and to allow for an initial assessment of competitive advantage. This matrix allows the evaluation of the costs and risks of launching the product against the costs and risks of opening up the market (Figure 8.5).

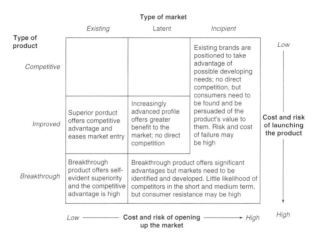

Fig. 8.5. Product/market combinations and the scope for competitive advantage on market entry
Source: Gilligan and Hird (1985)

Assessing the attractiveness of markets

The Figure 8.6 on the matrix indicate the likely order of priority in terms of market entry.

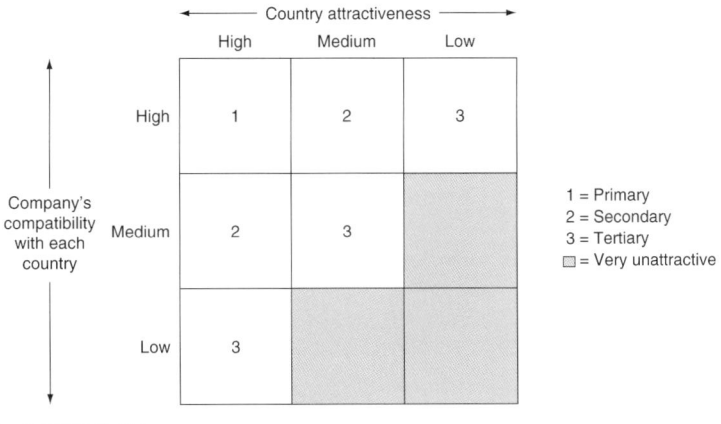

Fig. 8.6. Business portfolio matrix
Source: Harell and Keifer (1993)

Primary markets

- The markets falling in the top left hand corner, i.e., highly attractive and highly compatible, are likely to offer the best opportunities for long-term investment

Secondary markets

- These markets fall into the second tranche of priority since they are hampered by a medium attractiveness or medium compatibility score

Tertiary markets

- These are likely to be opportunistic markets at least in the short term

The International Marketing Intelligence System

A systematic method for gathering the data to allow the evaluation of candidate markets is required, i.e., a Marketing Intelligence System (MIS).

- To be effective there must be an effective communication channel between the environment in which the company operates and the decision makers
- An effective MIS provides a solid base for strategic decisions to be made
- The 12 C framework for analysis of international markets is shown in Figure 8.7 to give a structure to the data you should collect before deciding on target countries

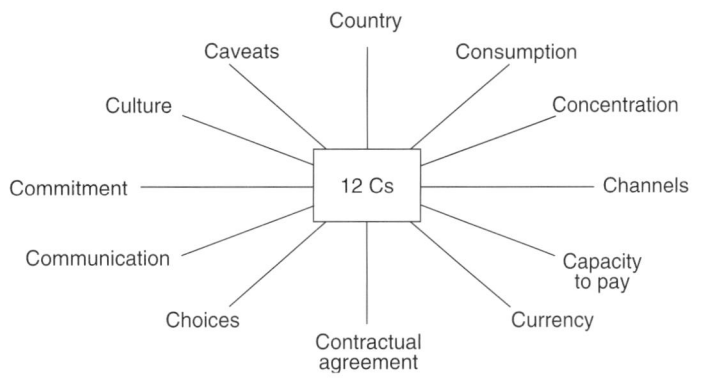

Fig. 8.7. The 12 Cs
Source: Doole and Lowe (1993)

An alternative way to assess market potential in emerging markets is offered by Cavusgil (1997). He also uses a weighted composite score and a variety of dimensions (Figure 8.8).

Dimension	Weight (out of 50)	Potential measures
Market size	10	○ Urban population ○ Electricity consumption
Market growth rate	6	○ Average annual growth rate of commercial energy use ○ Real GDP growth rate
Market intensity	7	○ GNI per capita estimates using PPP ○ Private consumption as a % of GDP
Market consumption capacity	5	○ % share of middle class in consumption/income
Commercial infrastructure	7	○ Phone lines (per 100 inhabitants) ○ Mobile phones (per 100 inhabitants) ○ No. of PCs (per 100 inhabitants) ○ Paved road density (km per million people) ○ Internet hosts (per million people) ○ Population per retail outlet ○ TVs per 1000 people

Fig. 8.8. Dimensions, weights and measures used to assess market potential

Dimension	Weight (out of 50)	Potential measures
Economic freedom	5	○ Economic Freedom Index ○ Political Freedom Index
Market receptivity	6	○ Per capita imports from the US ○ Trade as a percentage of GDP
Country risk	4	○ Country risk rating

Fig. 8.8. Continued

Market entry methods

By the time an organization has to make this decision, it will already have made three others:

1. To market internationally
2. Where to market
3. What to market

The next stage addresses how to determine the best way of entering the chosen market to optimize the potential of the chosen product range.

Factor	Comment
Corporate objectives, ambitions, resources	Will narrow the options but not necessarily to one
Nature of the market, product category, competition	Need to know scale, number, nature and level
Nature of consumer culture	What, where, how, why and how often consumers buy
Coverage of the market	Breadth, depth and quality, dictated by consumer need
Speed of entry	Nature of product, diffusion of innovation, stage in PLC, pace of market development
Level of control	Feedback required, research information to assess effectiveness
Marketing costs	Commitment increases as these get higher
Profit payback	Paybacks tend to take longer overseas. How long will the company wait?
Investment costs	Commitment increases as these get higher
Administrative requirements	Documentation, legal requirements, foreign taxation
Personnel	Level, training, language, assimilation
Flexibility	Testing before heavy involvement, multiple entry modes, ease of exit

Fig. 8.9. Determinants of level of involvement

Market entry strategy alternatives

When we are talking about market entry strategies we essentially have two main routes. We can either

- Make it here and sell it there, i.e., export, requiring relatively little involvement or
- Make it there and sell it there, i.e., overseas production, requiring a greater level of involvement

Figure 8.10 sets out the main strategic routes with the choice of entry modes listed under each.

Fig. 8.10. Market entry alternatives

To make the decision on mode of entry strategy an organization needs to address three factors:

1. What are the resources and investment necessary to enter the market?

2. To what extent does the organization want to control corporate activities in the foreign market?

3. How much knowledge can the organization gain by using this entry mode?

Figure 8.11 emphasizes the interaction between these factors on the choice of entry strategy.

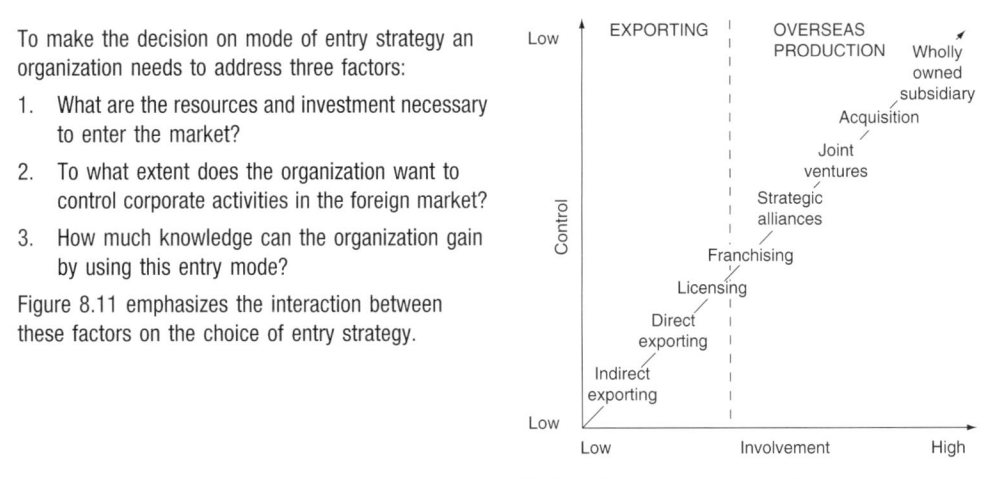

Fig. 8.11. Factors in assessment of entry modes

Culture

The development of international marketing strategies is based on a sound understanding of the similarities and differences that exist in countries around the world (Figure 8.12).

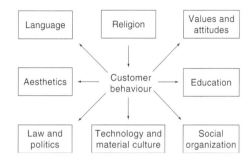

Fig. 8.12. The components of culture
Source: Adapted from Terpstra and Sarathy (2000)

Role of IT

Much has been made of the role of IT and in particular the internet in opening up the global marketplace.

According to Orlikowski (2000), companies use IT in three ways:

1. Reinforcing the status quo – These companies use IT to retain their existing ways of doing things.

2. Enhancing the status quo – These companies use IT to augment, improve and refine their existing work processes.

3. Transforming the status quo – These companies treat IT as a philosophy and use IT to alter substantially their existing ways of doing business.

Hints and tips

■ Examiners will expect you to demonstrate understanding of the global marketplace

■ Try to gain a detailed understanding of a sample of other countries. Keep a folder on each of your chosen countries. It helps to take one developed country and one less developed one as a minimum. Compare and contrast your chosen countries

■ Keep a file on the internet. What are the trends? How are organizations using the internet to market themselves. Keep examples of good practice, and bad. You can learn from both of them

DEFINING COMPETITIVE ADVANTAGE

LEARNING OUTCOMES

In this unit you will:

➡ Develop an understanding of the sources of competitive advantage.

➡ Identify the implications of the external and internal analyses for the company's strategic direction.

➡ Appreciate the importance of buyer behaviour in defining competitive advantage.

➡ After completing this unit you will be able to:

  ■ Define a source of competitive advantage for an organization.

  ■ Be able to plan scenarios effectively.

  ■ Assess the risk implicit in decision making.

KEY DEFINITIONS

Competitive advantage is the means by which a company can outperform its competitors and earn higher than average profits.

Core competence is something which the company does or possesses which gives it an edge over its competitors. It can be defined as the skills and technologies that enable the company to provide a particular benefit to customers. It may be a source of competitive advantage.

Scenario planning is the identification of a diverse range of potential futures.

What is competitive advantage?

- Competitive advantage is the means by which a company can outperform its competitors and earn higher than average profits
- The problem with competitive advantage is that competitors have an irritating habit of copying it
- Managers need to discourage this as much as possible. The two most common barriers to entry are brands and core competencies based on organizational effectiveness

Core competence

- This an be defined as the skills and technologies that enable the company to provide a particular benefit to customers. To be a core competence,

the following three criteria must be met:

1. Customer value – A core competence must make a disproportionate contribution to customer-perceived value.'

2. Competitive differentiation – If a competence is widely spread throughout an industry, it should not count as core unless the firm is demonstrably superior to that of its competitors.

3. Extendibility – It must be capable of leading to a wide array of new products and services.

Sustainable

- A successful competitive advantage is sustainable, not transitory. It should not be easily copied because the company wants to hold on to it for a long-term

Fit with external environment

- A competitive advantage derives not only from competitors' weaknesses (and therefore your strengths, but also from the market and conditions. Environmental dynamics can throw up threats and opportunities over time

- A well-thought-out SWOT analysis is invaluable here. The changes in the environment will happen anyway – there is nothing you can do to stop them. The trick is to be prepared for them and to adapt to them

Route to above-average profits

- The purpose of developing a competitive advantage is to earn above-average (for the industry) profits. Competitive advantage has an underlying assumption that the advantage is the result of past and present activity, and that it delivers (potentially at least) superior profits. However, competitors will be striving constantly to match and overtake the advantage, so the superior profits must be reinvested to stay ahead. The source–position–performance (SPP) model summarizes this process (Figure 9.1).

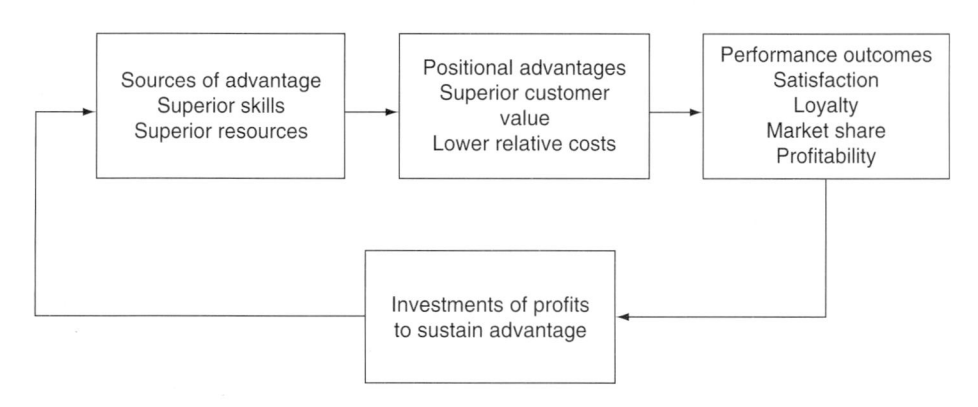

Fig. 9.1. The source–position–performance (SPP) model of competitive advantage
Source: Day and Wensley (1988)

Sources of advantage

- The ability of a company to do things better than its direct competitors arises from superior skills or superior resources. The competitors are usually those in the strategic group in which we are competing for our served market

Superior skills

- These stem from the ability of people in the firm to carry out certain tasks at a superior level. This assumes a generalized capability that does not depend on single individuals, and that can be maintained over time (though it may need support and reinvestment to do so)

Superior resources

- Resources may be financial or physical: ready availability of cash, for example, location, a state-of-the-art manufacturing plant

Positions of advantage

- Positional advantage is delivered by the sources, and may be either superior customer value or lower relative costs. Both can be understood within the framework of the value chain popularized by Porter (1985). Porter's generic strategies of differentiation and low cost mirror the two categories of advantage

- Competitive advantage (see Figure 9.2) delivers to target customers an offer that they perceive as providing superior value to the offers of competitors. Customers will buy the best value as they see it

Their perception of value can be broken down into three elements, as shown in Figure 9.2.

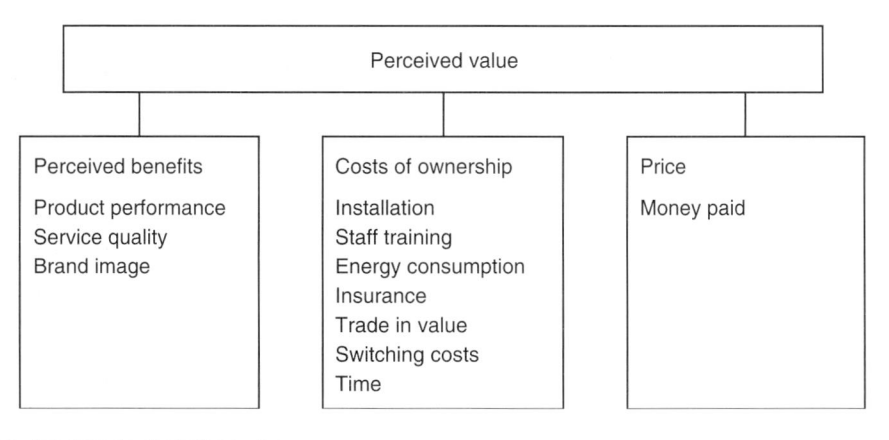

Fig. 9.2. Determinants of perceived value

Methods for assessing advantage

■ Advantage can be assessed from a competitor-centred or customer-focused assessment, or both. It is preferable to use both, as any one method will address only a part of the total picture.

Competitor-centred	Customer-focused

A. Assessing sources (distinctive competences)
    1. Management judgments of strengths and weaknesses
    2. Comparison of resource and capabilities
    3. Marketing skills audit
B. Indicators of positional advantage
    4. Competitive cost and activity comparisons
        a. Value chain comparisons of relative costs
        b. Cross-section experience curves
	
	5. Customer comparisons of attributes of firm
	   versus competitors
	   a. Choice models
	   b. Conjoint analysis
	   c. Market maps

Fig. 9.3. Methods of assessing advantage

Competitor-centred	Customer-focused

C. Identify key success factors

     6. Comparison of winning versus losing competitors

     7. Identifying high leverage phenomena

        a. Management estimates of market share elasticities

        b. Drivers of activities in the value chain

D. Measure of performance

	8. Customer satisfaction surveys
	9. Loyalty (customer franchise)
10a. Market share	10b. Relative share of end-user segments
11. Relative profitability	
(return on sales and return on assets)	

Fig. 9.3. Continued

Source: Day and Wensley (1988)

Porter's generic strategies

■ The best-known advocate of generic strategies has been Michael Porter. Porter (1980) set out three generic strategies, although he later subdivided the third (Figure 9.4). Porter argued that only the generic strategies – cost leadership, differentiation or focus – would lead to success

■ Companies that try to use a mixed strategy (cost leadership and differentiation, for example), would be 'stuck in the middle'. This idea that a successful strategy demands a single-minded focus has been a lasting and influential one ('stick to the knitting'), although Porter has become less dogmatic on this

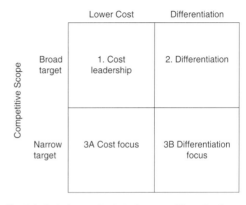

Fig. 9.4. Porter's generic strategies competitive advantage
Source: Porter (1985)

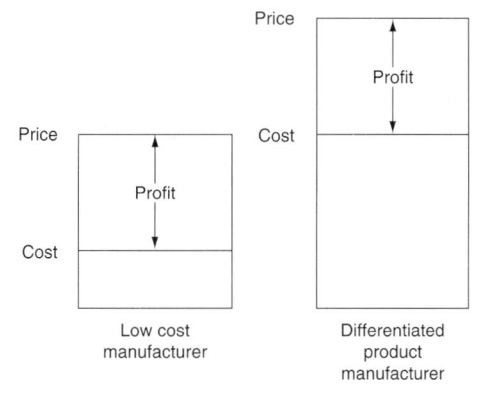

■ Profit is obviously the differential between price and cost, so above-average profit can be earned either by charging a premium price (and accepting a higher cost for producing a differentiated product) or by keeping costs low (and often accepting a lower price for your product). These two extremes can be viewed as the two ends of a spectrum, with companies occupying positions along it

Fig. 9.5. An example of competitive advantage
Source: Porter (1985)

Overall cost leadership

This strategy has the following advantages:

- Reduced bargaining power of suppliers, as high-volume production generated by low prices will lead to your holding large accounts with the manufacturers.

- Reduced bargaining power of customers – customers have little room to bargain against the company selling at the lowest prices.

- The two dangers for a company following a cost-leadership strategy are the entry of even lower-cost producers and a reduction in flexibility.

Differentiation strategy

- A strategy of differentiation is concerned with making the intangible and/or tangible aspects of a product different from those offered by other sellers

- Firms sell unique products in the hope of building a franchise among less price-sensitive buyers. The reduced price sensitivity, and hence the higher price charged, tends to lead to higher profits

The elements of product quality, product innovation, style and image are all important factors in creating differentiation. Differentiation as a strategy has a number of advantages:

- Reduced bargaining power of consumers. The differences between products mean that products are not directly comparable – the consumer either has to pay the price or settle for something different

- Substitutes are less attractive because they are not direct substitutes

■ Reduced competition, because differentiation creates a series of monopolistic submarkets

Focus strategy

■ The strategy relates to companies that specialize in a certain segment of the market. There is considerable overlap between this type of segmentation and that of differentiation strategy. Segmentation focuses on the market and differentiation on the product differences

■ A focus strategy has the following advantages:
   1. Reduced competition, by meeting the needs of a particular segment rather than the larger market.
   2. Reduced pressure from substitutes. Its main problems occur by being dependent on just one segment, and by being successful and enlarging the segment, other, larger manufacturers may be attracted into it.

Day's matrix

Day proposed a similar model (Figure 9.6), using customer price sensitivity and real or perceived differences in the product offering as the axes.

	Small	Large
High	Overall cost leadership Flat steel Refined sugar Cement Gasoline	Differentiation (Seek major quality or structural differences) Earth-moving machinery Mainframe computers Major appliances
Low	Hybrid (Low cost and emphasize differences) Home insulation Fine abrasives Chewing gum	Focus (Search for real or perceived differences) Credit services News magazines Food additives

Customer price sensitivity

Real or perceived relative differences in product offerings

Fig. 9.6. Day's matrix
Source: Day (1984)

How to use generic strategies

■ Generic strategies are best viewed as a framework within which to think about the strategic possibilities for an organization

■ Use the generic strategies as a first step in the process of developing a strategy, but do not be tied by them. Use them creatively and adapt them to your own business and its environment

■ As with all general business models, the generic strategy approach has been subject to criticism. In particular, it has been pointed out that some companies are successful while combining supposedly incompatible strategies. Increasingly, low cost has become an absolute essential rather than an option

Scenario planning

■ Scenario planning is all about identifying a diverse range of potential futures. This can be done by the senior management group, the whole company, with external people, or whatever. The important thing is that the group has alternative perspectives to offer and that all are familiar with the environmental analysis which has already been undertaken

■ A simple approach involves the following four steps:
  1. Identify the critical variables – The long-term drivers of the business should be identified and evaluated on the basis of their importance to the business and the level of certainty associated with their direction.
  2. Develop possible strings of events – The key drivers of change are those which are important but not predictable.

3. Refine the scenarios – At the end of stage 2, there should be a range of scenarios, some of these will be more believable than others. The group needs to assess the potential scenarios on the grounds of internal consistency, credibility and recognizability.

4. Identify the issues arising – Those scenarios which survive need to be reviewed – Have any critical events or outcomes been identified, which would have a major impact on the organization?.

Assessing risk

■ All strategic options carry an element of risk as the future is uncertain. Our scenario planning carries with it an explicit or implicit prediction of the activities of many groups, but particularly those of customers and competitors. All of these have an element of unpredictability

■ The Ansoff matrix can be used to determine the general level of risk. Continuing in existing markets is likely to offer the lowest level of risk since the organization is familiar both with the market and the technology. Market development and new product development, each add to the risk by adding newness; the first in terms of the customer base and the second in terms of technology

■ The fourth option within the Ansoff classification is diversification, which is generally accepted as the most risky as it involves a leap in the unknown in terms of marketing and technological knowledge

■ Aaker (1998) suggests the following responses to uncertainty on (Figure 9.7) dependent on the likely immediacy and potential impact.

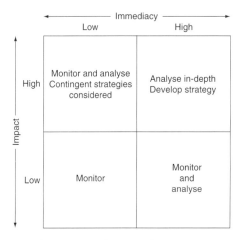

Fig. 9.7. Strategic uncertainty categories
Source: Aaker (1998, p. 109)

■ Strategy is defined as the set of decisions taken to determine how an organization allocates its resources and achieves sustainable competitive advantage in those markets. Its sources are superior skills and superior resources, which deliver the positional advantages of superior customer value and lower relative costs

■ These link to Porter's generic strategies of differentiation and cost leadership. The performance outcomes of these advantages are of enhanced market share and profitability

Hints and tips

■ Examiners are interested in your ability to see the strategic implications of your analysis. Since we cannot change the past, the future is important. Practise your ability to plan alternative future scenarios which are logically based on your analysis. Include a sensitivity analysis which allows the company to make strategic decisions effectively

■ Return to the learning outcomes listed in Unit 1. Remember that the examiners will be assessing you on these. Make sure that you feel comfortable with your ability to demonstrate each of these

BIBLIOGRAPHY

Aaker, D.A., Kumar, V., Day G.S. (1997) Marketing Research, John Wiley & Sons.

Ansoff, I. (1988) Corporate Strategy, Penguin Books, Harmondsworth.

Carter, S. (2004) International Marketing Strategy (2004–2005), Butterworth Heinemann.

Day, G.S. (1984) Strategic Market Planning: The Pursuit of Competitive Advantage, West Publishing, Minneapolis.

Day, G.S. and Wensley, R. (1988) 'Assessing Advantage: A Framework Published by American Marketing Association for Diagnosing Competitive Superiority', Journal of Marketing, 52, April, pp. 1–20.

Doole, I. and Lowe, R. (1999) Strategic Marketing Decisions in Global Markets, Thomson Learning.

Doyle, P. (1994) Marketing Management and Strategy, Prentice-Hall International, Hemel Hempstead.

Gillligan, C. and Hird, M. (1986) International Marketing, Croom Helm.

Gurden, D. (2001) 'In Internet World', Mecklermedia Corporation, Westport, Conn.

Hall Edward, T. (1976) Beyond Culture, New York, Anchor Press.

Hamel, G. and Prahalad, C.K. (1996) Competing for the Future, Harvard Business School Press, Boston, MA.

Harrell, G.D. and Kiefer, R.O. (1993) 'Multinational Market Portfolios in Global Strategy Development', International Marketing Review, 10(1), pp. 60–72.

Johnson, G. and Scholes, K. (1997) Exploring Corporate Strategy, Prentice-Hall International, Hemel Hempstead.

Narver, John C. and Stanley F. Slater (1990) 'The Effect of a Market Orientation on Business Profitability', Journal of Marketing, 54, October, pp. 20–35.

Ohmae, K. (1982) The Mind of Strategist: The Art of Japanese Business, McGraw-Hill.

Parasuraman, Zeithaml and Berry, 'A Conceptual Model of Service Quality and Its Implications for Future Research', Journal of Marketing, Fall, 1985, pp. 41–50.

Porter, M.E. (1980) Competitive Strategy: Techniques for Analysing Industries and Competitors, Free Press, New York.

Porter, M.E. (1985) Competitive Advantage: Creating and Sustaining Superior Performance, Free Press, New York.

Robert S. Kaplan, et al. (1996) Balanced Scorecard: Translating Strategy into Action, Harvard Business School Press.

Terpstra, R. and Sarathy (Editors) (2000) International Marketing, The Dryden Press.

Usunier, J.-C. (1998) International and Cross-Cultural Management Research, Sage.